Locative Social Media

Locative Social Media

Place in the Digital Age

Leighton Evans
National University of Ireland Maynooth, Ireland

First published 2015 by
PALGRAVE MACMILLAN

Palgrave Macmillan in the UK is an imprint of Macmillan Publishers Limited, registered in England, company number 785998, of Houndmills, Basingstoke, Hampshire, RG21 6XS.

Palgrave Macmillan in the US is a division of St Martin's Press LLC, 175 Fifth Avenue, New York, NY 10010.

Palgrave is a global academic imprint of the above companies and has companies and representatives throughout the world.

Palgrave® and Macmillan® are registered trademarks in the United States, the United Kingdom, Europe and other countries.

ISBN 978–1–137–45610–6

This book is printed on paper suitable for recycling and made from fully managed and sustained forest sources. Logging, pulping and manufacturing processes are expected to conform to the environmental regulations of the country of origin.

A catalogue record for this book is available from the British Library.

A catalog record for this book is available from the Library of Congress.

Typeset by MPS Limited, Chennai, India.

For my parents; their support has made this possible.

Contents

List of Figures

Acknowledgements

This book began as a PhD project at Swansea University, supervised by Dr David M. Berry, with co-supervision by Dr Ieuan Williams and Dr Mario von der Ruhr. I owe sincere thanks to David, who made me believe in myself and guided me through the whole process of writing the original thesis. I am sure that this book would not have been possible without his support, inspiration, understanding and encouragement throughout and his great ability to assist and help direct my thoughts and reading. Other colleagues at Swansea University have provided incredibly valuable support, and I wish to thank William Merrin, Yan Wu, Mostyn Jones, Sian Rees, Faustin Changombie and Peter Black for their help and comments. In particular, I thank David Clarke and Jussi Parikka who reviewed this book in an early form as a PhD thesis and provided useful recommendations for revisions.

I received considerable assistance from other researchers and academics throughout this research. In particular I would like to thank Katina Michael for all her support, help and advice. Glen Farrelly, Michael Saker and Phil Adams were key contemporaries at Swansea and I look forward to their books on the similar material.

The completion of this book was made possible while in receipt of funding from the European Research Council as part of the Programmable City project at Maynooth University (grant: ERC-2012-AdG 323636-SOFTCITY). My thanks go to Professor Rob Kitchin, and to the team at Maynooth who have offered support and advice. In particular, I thank Mark Boyle, Robert Bradshaw, Alan Moore, Darach MacDonncha, Jim White, Sophia Maalsen, Sung-Yueh Perng and Tracey Lauriault.

1
Introduction

The research underpinning the analysis and argument of this book originated from my interest in how technology interfaced with everyday life in science-fiction. I cannot think of any book that has such an influence on my perspective of the world as *Neuromancer*, the canonical novel of cyberspace and hackers by William Gibson, published in 1984. The book and the world that Gibson created in *Neuromancer* fascinates not just for precedence, but also for the uncomfortable, uncanny feeling that the present is reworked in a manner that estranges familiarity (see Kitchin and Kneale, 2005). Gibson's vision is of a world where human beings and networked digital technology co-exist and perception of the world is dependent upon the co-existence and use of computational devices. The co-existence often borders on the hostile, but is also a way of understanding the how the world is made sense of by the characters in the book in a world imbued with and dominated by information, data and computer technology.

On reflection what was so striking about *Neuromancer* was the way that the place of action in the book – be that Chiba City, the Sprawl or cyberspace itself – was articulated by the writer. The book is challenging to understand, as the neologisms Gibson uses to create a sense of place in these locations are so jarringly new to the first time reader. The experience is disorientating; one struggles to understand and to form a mental picture of settings:

> Program a map to display frequency of data exchange, every thousand megabytes a single pixel on a very large screen. Manhattan and Atlanta burn solid white. Then they start to pulse, the rate of traffic threatening to overload your simulation. Your map is about to go nova. Cool it down. Up your scale. Each pixel a million megabytes.

At a hundred million megabytes per second, you begin to make out certain blocks in midtown Manhattan, outlines of hundred-year-old industrial parks ringing the old core of Atlanta. (Gibson, 1984: 43)

This is a description of the Sprawl, an endless city stretching from modern-day Boston down the East coast to Atlanta and beyond, but a city in the singular, one continuous urban landscape. Gibson forces the reader to understand the place of action through what was, at the time of his writing, an alien real-time cartographic technique, using pulses of data to represent place rather than the geographic features or gazetteers in maps one would have been accustomed to in 1984. In doing so, Gibson is using a heuristic technique to give the sense of scale of place quickly in the narrative, but the experience is one of estrangement for the reader and protagonist. The protagonist (Case, the anti-hero hacker at the centre of the narrative) attunes himself to this view as if it were normal (as one might now do, 30 years later). It is how Case *sees* places, understands them and dwells within them:

He looked around the deserted dead end street. A sheet of newsprint went cartwheeling past the intersection. Freak winds in the East side; something to do with convection, and an overlap in the domes. Case peered through the window at the dead sign. Her sprawl wasn't his sprawl, he decided. She'd led him through a dozen bars and clubs he'd never seen before, taking care of business, usually with no more than a nod. Making connections. (Gibson, 1984: 8)

Here, Case is unfamiliar in a particular part of the vast Sprawl, while his companion Molly is at home, or familiar, with that place. That one can feel at home in the Sprawl is something that did not surprise me, as anyone that has lived in a city knows. You acquire familiarity with the places you frequent most often and a feeling of being at home in them without necessarily becoming familiar with the city as a whole. In the undifferentiated urban landscapes Gibson describes, people connect with people and places, such as bars and junk stores, as well as online. In these situations the characters go from the confusing and unsettlingly fast-paced Sprawl into familiar places that have a sense of place and community. Through a process of reading, thinking and empathising, the reader also becomes familiar, with both the urban and cyber landscapes that are described, as one becomes accustomed to the objects, things and technology that Gibson uses to describe his places. What appears bewildering is understood through the things that he uses to explain place. The entire place of the novel unfolds and makes sense once one understands the technology and objects Gibson uses to create place within the narrative (for further reading see Batty, 1997a; Concannon, 1998; Myers, 2001). The world in the book is not far removed from the world we find ourselves in today: an environment often dominated and defined by computational devices. Gibson offers a fictional view of how users could become attuned to a world that is populated by such devices, and how humans make sense of places in terms of their relationships mediated by such devices.

In 2007, I read (out of morbid curiosity) "Industrial Society and Its Future" by the Unabomber, Ted Kaczynski (2005). His manifesto describes a system (of technological objects and technology) that "does not exist to satisfy human needs," but rather "human behaviour has to be modified to fit the needs of the system." The system described is not guided by ideology but by technological necessity, a form of techno-logical determinism. In this description of technicity, when you engage with any part of the technological world you are not released by it; you are kept in a reserve by the technological world, having to use it again and use it more, and use other technology until you are absorbed by technology. While the Unabomber was judged to be insane, and his criminal campaign of murder thankfully ended, his vision of technology as a totalising, autonomous system is an influential idea not alien to the field of philosophy of technology. This book explores the notion of tech-nological control and totalisation in a world filled with computational devices – but does not share the Unabomber's scepticism. While there is no doubt that we live alongside and increasingly use technology (and here I refer to digital, computational technology) in our everyday living, I will argue that (even through the utilisation of philosophical ideas associated with technological control and domination) the use of digital technology in everyday navigation of the world can both deepen under-standing of place and reduce place to commodity. The direction of this is a function of the mood of the user, rather than the technology itself.

The focus of analysis is specifically concerned with mobile devices and the relatively new phenomenon of location-based social net-working (LBSN). In 2011, IMS research predicted that 420 million smartphones – small, powerful mobile computing devices carried daily – would be sold in globally in 2011, rising to one billion in 2016, which would constitute half the global mobile phone market (IMS Research, 2011). In 2013, half of 12- to 17-year-olds in America owned a smart-phone (Madden et al., 2013). This proliferation of mobile computing is creating a world of continual computational presence. Even Gibson had Case jacking into the Internet at a fixed console, and while the experience of the Internet is not totally embodied (as yet) as Gibson envisaged, the presence of information and computation on the move is certainly present for those that choose to use their smartphones or tablets. This is the technology that people are using more and more on a daily basis to access email, surf the Internet, use social networking and locate themselves in the world.[1]

I originally questioned the value of embedding Global Positioning System technology (GPS) within mobile handsets. I began to understand their utility, however, with the emergent practices that coalesced around Foursquare and Gowalla, two LBSN platforms, particularly at the South by Southwest (SXSW) music festival in January 2010. SXSW seemed to be a focal point for an emergent use of GPS in phones, as people tagged themselves (or their devices) to a venue or band playing at that venue. Membership numbers on Foursquare and Gowalla at that time were exploding. What is of importance is what these programmes asked users to do. Twitter, Facebook and others already ask users to share their thoughts with the members of their social network and what they are doing and why they are doing it. Location-based social networks not only do this, but also ask the user to share the exact location of where they are doing this activity.

Location-based services (LBSs) are the fastest growing sector in web-based technology business (Gordon and de Souza e Silva, 2011: 9). These services, be they LBSN, satellite navigation devices in cars or augmented reality browsers as applications on mobile phones, open questions about the awareness of location and engagement with location for users. McCullogh (2006: 26) argues that LBSs are a channel or means of obtaining hyper-specialised information, in that the information reaching users is now about where they are, rather than decontextualised information with no relevance to their location. The use of LBSN is an extension of the use of GPS technology for everyday use, but whereas the GPS used in in-car systems is based on a database of places owned and licensed commercially by the manufacturer, LBSNs build their databases of places through the use of the service by the users themselves – crowdsourcing the database. Users "create" the place, they check in (denoting presence at a place through the application) and comment, creating gazetteers of location, type and personal opinion within an open and freely available network. As I began to use this technology in 2010, I firstly began to explore the gamification[2] of LBSN and the collection of 'game' points within the game.[3] Moreover, when using the application Foursquare in unfamiliar places, for example when travelling to academic conferences or for weekends away, I found that I could use the recommendations and patterns of use of other users to inform my own movements. In effect, I was using the LBSN to *navigate my way through unfamiliar space, and in doing this I was gaining familiarity* – restaurants, bars, taxi ranks, places of interest, all became visible through the interface. On a trip to London in March 2010, unfamiliar spaces did become meaningful places largely through the use of the LBSN Foursquare. In using the LBSN in this way, I was using a user-generated map full of social gazetteers created entirely by other users and how they understood the places that were around me. My understanding of place was an orientation of myself to the understanding of place shared with me as a member of the LBSN, and mapped by other users.

This type of mapping is in agreement with Deleuze and Guattari's (in Shaviro, 2010: 7) concepts of what maps are: tools for negotiating in and intervening in social space rather than static representations of territory. Maps therefore do not replicate the shape of a territory; rather they inflect and represent that territory in a particular way (see Chapter 2 of this volume) – a distinction between ontic and ontogenetic representation of space. LBSNs allow maps to be realised not just in creation but also in distribution to anyone that owns a suitable computational device using the Internet. With Foursquare installed, the user can use maps in negotiation with the environment, charting their movements and thoughts as an overlay on that map which is in itself an overlay over the physical territory. In this sense they are like Borges' famous tale from "Of Exactitude in Science":

> In that Empire, the craft of Cartography attained such perfection that the Map of a single province covered the space of an entire City, and the Map of the Empire itself an entire Province. In the course of time, these extensive maps were found somehow wanting, and so the college of Cartographers evolved a Map of the Empire that was of the same scale as the Empire and that coincided with it point for point. Less attentive to the study of Cartography, succeeding generations came to judge a map of such magnitude cumbersome, and, not without irreverence, they abandoned it to the rigours of sun and rain. In the western Deserts, tattered Fragments of the map are still to be found, sheltering an occasional beast or beggar; in the whole nation, no other relic is left of the Discipline of Geography. (Borges, 1998: 325)

My reading of Borges is that the map of the Empire cannot be used in a negotiation of the type that Deleuze and Guattari describe; when the map is purely a representation of the territory, it is an impossibility, instead requiring abstraction, generalisation, editing and "formatting" – in effect simplification. Mapping is a way of making inscriptions of meaning that assist in the navigation of the world, and this is what Foursquare and other LBSN encourage, in line with Verhoeff's (2012: 13) argument that in a world where screens are ubiquitous, navigation becomes a primary trope in urban mobility and visibility.

The situation is that the technology available to us – inexpensive, easy to use and with free and open mapping technology – has allowed almost anyone to use maps to negotiate and navigate a world, and to contribute to the navigation practices of others. There is a shift in the role of cartographer from skilled mapmaker to digital database manager, through the triangulation of LBSN, technology and user. The technology facilitates the urge to map through its presence and the practices of doing so offers an understanding of place for the user that is different from the use of a traditional map. Jameson (1991: 89–92) understood the need for maps as a technology that enables the understanding of the world. Citing Lynch's (1960) *The Image of the City*, Jameson argues that spaces that people *become unable to map are alienated spaces*; spaces that cannot be understood in the minds of people. Jameson understands social cartography as having the consequence of endowing the individual subject with a heightened sense of place in the global system (Jameson, 1991: 90). Social cartography is not understood in this context as a reorganisation of older forms of mapping, but as a means of *understanding and regaining a capacity to act in a world* that the modern subject is spatially confused by through the neutralisation of spatiality through technological representation. The cognitive mapping that Jameson advocates is a form of taking up place through practices that are attuned to social behaviours and understanding of place through the social and practical aspects of place. Particular practices of being involved with technology produce a *poetic understanding of place*. This is not to say that technological representations of place cannot lead to instrumental understandings of place, however. Ultimately, the argument I advance aims to understand what practices of use are indicative of and essential to deeper understandings of place or instrumental understandings in the digital age through an exploration of location-based social media usage.

Space and place

The concepts of space and place are obviously important in this project. Newton distinguished between two kinds of space: absolute space and relative space. Absolute space is always the same and immutable, without reference of any other points of reference and with no requirement for anything to fill that space (Jacobson, 2006: 15). Absolute space has no secondary qualities such as colour, shape or extension, and as such has no substance or recognisable quality that allows for human comprehension through the senses. In contrast, relative space – marked-off portions of absolute space – has the kind of features for spatial understanding that humans have in everyday epistemology. A university campus for example would be relative space, with discernible boundaries, and something that could be divided further to signify other spaces within that larger relative space e.g. a building, a lecture theatre, an office, a storage cupboard. The number of possible relative spaces is limitless, and these spaces can overlap one another e.g. one has an office (a relative space) within a building (another relative space) (Jacobson, 2006: 16).

For Newton, space exists independently of human beings, and is not dependent upon human beings for its existence or intelligibility. Newton's reasons for this view were to provide an objective foundation for spatiality through which his laws of motion could be made intelligible and understandable through mathematical principles, which is why absolute space is necessarily apart from human interpretation or action. Humans cannot perceive an object's position in absolute space because absolute space cannot be understood through perception, only through notions of Euclidian space and mathematical principles (Jacobson, 2006: 18). In this view, then, humans are not directly in contact with absolute space at all, only interpreting that absolute space relatively through cognitive processes. Relative space becomes a function of the understanding of points between objects and therefore subjective and dependent upon sensation. What we might term place – that is, sites of human activity such as the building or office – is the use of the intellect to make sense of space in a meaningful way. Here, I use Heidegger's notion of place as a meaningful existential locale made up of a referential totality of things in that location that gives meaning to the location, rather than an undifferentiated locale which would be space. This position is explained at length in Chapter 3.

Descartes' concept of spatiality is similar to Newton's, but also differs in some significant ways. Most significantly, for Descartes there cannot be empty spaces as all space is filled with extended bodies, or *res extensa* (Jacobson, 2006: 23), and space is the accumulation of these bodies (Descartes, 1997: 49). Space is extension and matter is indistinguishable from space, and therefore all space must necessarily be filled with matter. For Descartes all space can be is matter, and nothing else.[4] This difference between Descartes and Newton has significance as it allows for the possibility of a space that is defined by things that constitute that space, and that space itself and the space that is perceived are the same thing (Jacobson, 2006: 24). Descartes qualifies this difference in his analysis of the senses in the *Meditations* (1997: 38). Famously, Descartes claims that the senses can deceive as part of his attempt to defeat scepticism and find a ground for certainty. As a stick can appear bent in water (through refraction) we must not (according to Descartes) trust the senses at all. This line of argument eventually concludes in the *cogito* as the only certainty that Descartes can have against scepticism, and the eventual substance dualism that separates extended matter from mental substance (the mind) ontologically in Descartes philosophy. This is critical for the understanding of space in Descartes' philosophy. Space, as matter, cannot be encountered directly even though things and matter constitute this space.

So, in these conceptions of space, space is something that is perceived by the mind through the senses and body that is also material but which the mind "inhabits" – albeit, in a confusing way.[5] The contact between the thinking *thing* (a human) and space is not only indirect but also subject to error and misjudgement from using senses that can deceive, and therefore knowledge of space itself is uncertain. By making the mind necessarily separate from matter, Descartes orders the importance of spatiality and non-extended substance. Space is only extension, and while the body is part of that extension it is of secondary importance to the intellect in understanding extension; Descartes was certain that *he exists* and his role as a thinking thing is to think and understand the world. Understanding emerges from the operation of the intellect through the deduction of mathematical truths about space. While Descartes is willing to admit that space consists of something, unlike Newton, both theories contend that space is understood only as rational proofs and truths derived by the intellect that is necessarily separate from that space, and therefore cannot understand space through an engagement with or emergence within space.

In these theories, space is an independent entity that can only be known through the operation of the intellect that provides humans with rational rules and mathematical truths for understanding space properly. The human being does not exist in *space*; rather space exists around the human being, as an ocean of non-thinking substance that requires interpretation from the bubble of thinking stuff that is the human/mind/immaterial substance. The Cartesian idea of space as something separate from humans, understood only through rational reflection and mathematical rules does not resonate with the idea that technological objects can characterise space and aid understanding, and more than this provide a sense of place. This is due to the place afforded to humans in the Cartesian system: definitively apart from space, an immaterial observer and interpreter of matter but not in any way physically engaged with the matter that makes up space (as this would be logically incoherent).

In a phenomenological view, place is not as Descartes would argue, just undifferentiated matter, but is filled with things that provide meaning and a sense of differentiated *place* (Relph, 1976: 43) rather than undifferentiated *space*. Space is lived in (Elden, 2004: 187) rather than observed from outside. Descartes' understanding of space is not impossible, but it is not the only way of understanding space. Consider being "lost": the person is unfamiliar with the place, cannot orient himself or herself to it, and cannot understand that place. The abstraction of space by the device does not lend itself to understanding, but instead leads to bewilderment, as space is represented in an optimally efficient manner for navigation, without the means to familiarise oneself and become aware of the possibilities of danger in that space. The revealing of space in an overly efficient way is symptomatic of the technological revealing of place, place revealed only as space to be navigated. In effect, the user lacks what Jameson (1991: 83) terms a cognitive map: a way of understanding the space as a place and being able to move through that place.[6] The user is given a representation of space only as co-ordinates; space instrumentally presented and understood for the purpose of moving through, not dwelling within. This would correspond to a Cartesian understanding of space. On the other hand, a phenomenological account of space treats the human as not only a part of space, but necessarily in space, spatiality being not an abstract understanding of co-ordinates but a relation to other things in the world that one is in contact with and understands by standing in relation to, rather than understanding rationally from afar.

Therefore, drawing on the philosophy of Heidegger and others, I argue that the space can be better understood *phenomenologically*, through lived-in experience that comes from interacting with things in the world. This view of spatiality contends that by drawing objects into *care* (that is, by treating them with concern and as entities rather than mere extension) the thing orients people towards the world and provides an understanding of space. This understanding of things in the world leads to a dwelling in the world, where one understands space as a place that can be thought about, understood and where one can be at "home" in the world (Jacobson, 2006: 1) rather than simply view the world as a disengaged observer. In this place, the person is oriented to understanding spatiality as a meaningful relational orientation to other things in that place, where the meaning of the place is emergent from the totality of relations to the things found in that place. This understanding involves accepting Heidegger's rejection of the subject-object distinction in Descartes and the idea that the mind is separate from the world; in other words, humans are in the world necessarily, as opposed to outside of the world necessarily. In being-in-the-world, humans become at home through dwelling, and this dwelling is achieved through relationships with things that orient us in places and make them familiar.

Computationality

The modern world is one characterised by the increasing presence of computational technology in everyday life created a common doxa of the world as deeply computational – *computationality* (Berry, 2011). Technological objects can nonetheless provide *orientation* for humans to dwell in the world; the possibility that humans can be at home with technology. Heidegger's view of modern technology was that it alienated people from "authentic" being, by obscuring the view of things in the world as things and reducing them to pure objects to be used as resource through a revealing of efficiency and utility above any further meaning (Heidegger, 1977: 33). Although, of course, Heidegger believed that we would need to develop a free relation with technology to move beyond pure instrumentality, something Berry (2008) discusses in relation to the possibilities of building things in cooperation and at human scale. A pessimistic view of modern technology does not necessarily fit with the potential of computational devices, and these devices' capacity to reveal place as something other than resource, or simply co-ordinates to be understood rationally. An understanding of place as something non-instrumental and with meaning on a human scale comes from a resonance or attunement to place that comes from practices of using computational devices.[7]

Technological devices can reveal the world *poetically* rather than simply technologically, and this *poesis* is a consequence of taking the computational device into concern rather than treating it as an object to be used (see Berry, 2008: 188–201). A poetic revealing of the world is one where things and the world are revealed as being more than just resources to be used; as meaningful entities in an emergent referential totality called *place*. Heidegger argues that a technological revealing unveils things as resources to be used; place becomes space – something endlessly divisible, fixed and understood mathematically. In contrast, I present a view of modern technology that challenges many orthodox views within Heideggerian scholarship that hold that modern technology is viewed from within Heidegger's paradigm as a "danger" to the understanding of being itself by obliterating the place for understanding being through thinking. Rather, I argue that computational devices are not a *modern* technology, in the Heideggerian sense, rather it is something that can be a thing that "things" in the world to reveals a world as more than resource. The post-phenomenology (incorporating body and world into the base phenomenology influenced by Heidegger) I forward positions people's being-with the device as fundamentally different to previous technologies that simply measured, instrumentalised, formatted and purified. A computational device (for example, a smartphone) *can* reveal the world technologically, but can also reveal the world *poetically* and in doing so people can dwell with the device, be at home with it, as Case is at home in cyberspace and in the vast undifferentiated Sprawl, when technology orients man to make the space a place of meaning.

Software studies

The notion of software, computation, code and computational devices as key to understanding the world through their usage is not what one thinks of as computer science. Rather, my argument, which considers the phenomenological and post-phenomenological effects of digital computational devices on understanding place, is broadly positioned within the emerging area of software studies. This field is characterised by work that proposes that software can be seen as an object of study and an area of practice for kinds of thinking and areas of work that have not historically "owned" software, or indeed often had much to say about it. Such areas include those that are currently concerned with culture and media from the perspectives of politics, society and systems of thought and aesthetics or those that renew themselves via criticism, speculation and precise attention to events and to matter, among others (Fuller, 2008: 17).

Software studies is an interdisciplinary field that addresses software from an orientation not based in computer science or programming. The difference between software studies and those more broadly studying the digital technologies can be summarised by analogy (Dodge and

Kitchin, 2011: 18): it can be characterised as the difference between studying the underlying epidemiology of ill health and the effects of ill health on the world. While one can say a great deal about the relationship between health and society by studying broadly how ill health affects social relations, one can gain further insight by considering the specifics of different diseases, their aetiology (causes, origins, evolution and implications) and how these manifest themselves in shaping social relations. Software studies therefore focus on the aetiology of code and how code makes digital technologies what they are and shapes what they do. It seeks to open the black box of processors and arcane algorithms to understand how software – its lines and routines of code – does work in the world by instructing various technologies how to act (Dodge and Kitchin, 2011: 18).

The canonical works of the emerging field include Galloway's *Protocol* (2004); Fuller's *Behind the Blip* (2003) and *Software Studies: A Lexicon* (2008); Lessig's "Code and Other Laws of Cyberspace" (1999); Manovich's *The Language of New Media* (2000) and *Software Takes Command* (2013); Hayles's *My Mother Was a Computer* (2005); Berry's *The Philosophy of Software* (2011); Chun's *Programmed Visions* (2011); Dodge and Kitchin's *Code/Space* (2011); and Mackenzie's *Cutting Code* (2006). Manovich (2000: 48) argues that "to understand the logic of new media we need to turn to computer science. It is there that we may expect to find the new terms, categories and operations which characterise media which became programmable. From media studies, we move to something which can be called software studies; from media theory – to software theory."

The shift to software studies is therefore both an acknowledgement of the importance of software and an imperative to operationalise that acknowledgement in the methods, aims and objectives of the research done in the social sciences. This can be understood as an orientation to the social politics of software: how it is written and developed; how software does work in the world to produce new subjects, practices, mobilities, transactions and interactions; the nature of the software industry; and the social, economic, political and cultural consequences of code on different domains, such as business, health, education and entertainment (Dodge and Kitchin, 2011: 18). Software has become a putatively mature part of societal formations (or at least enters a phase where generations are now born into it as an infrastructural element of daily life), and social science needs to gather and make palpable a range of associations and interpretations of software to be understood and experimented with (Fuller, 2008: 18). Among other things, this course of study and orientation requires an emphasising of the neglected aspects of computation, which involve the possibilities of virtuality, simulation, abstraction, feedback and autonomous processes (Fuller, 2008: 19).

In essence, software has become our familiar (Fuller, 2008: 26). Software is entwined in our everyday lives and as such requires the attention of those people who seek to understand everyday lives in the same way that education, language, politics, technology or any other phenomenon that affects social change demands attention. For example: Hayles (2009: 48) notes the proliferation of Radio-Frequency Identification (RFID) technology in everyday objects, relaying location-based data, transforming objects in the world from passive and inert to active participants in their data provision and actions in the world. While this poses problems for notions of privacy, concentration on this aspect may lead to overlooking the possibility of reassessing embedded human action in complex environments. This possibility is a result of the trend of the movement of computation "out of the box and into the environment" (Hayles, 2009: 48) and towards a distributed cognition where small sub-cognisers performing limited ranges of operation are combined with readers that interpret that information linked to databases for storing that information. This is the "internet of things" (Gershenfeld, 1999; Hayles, 2009: 49). This research fits with this view of Internet-enabled mobile computational devices as part of a wider framework of devices that perform bespoke, discreet tasks in the world and affect subjectivity and human perception accordingly. Such insights go beyond instrumentalist views of technology and look to understand change and remediation of the world through the presence of software in the world.

Such an approach to media technology as causing alterations in human behaviour is part of a long tradition in theory, from McLuhan's (2008) arguments that media are an extension of man in the world and the medium is the message, when one wants to assess the effects of media on human behaviour and society, to Kittler's (1999) argument that media structures "human affairs" through the production, processing, transmission and storage of data. For example, Meyrowitz (1986) described how media technology (specifically television) has shaped and influenced social relations and eradicated "distance" between actors. He argued that television acts to disrupt notions of what it means to be present, and hence causes dislocations in social behaviour and the link between physical space and social place. Further, Postman (1985) contended that a particular form of media can only sustain a certain set of ideas, and therefore is limiting in how the world can be experienced, and cautions against utopian or even optimistic visions of what software in the world can achieve.

Strictly, such approaches and critiques should not be considered as software studies (not least due to the lack of software as a focus) but they are useful in historicising the field as a branch of critical theory that is concerned with how technology affects human understanding and existence in the world. Of more salience is the possibility of criticism on the grounds of technological determinism. If one considers the argument of Raymond Williams (2003), who contended that we have to think of determination not as a single force, or a single abstraction of forces, but as a process in which real determining factors set limits and exert pressures (Williams, 2003: 133), then software should be thought as a factor amongst others in the shaping of the world in which software is a factor. This is more broadly what software studies as a discipline does, and it achieves this through the retention and modification of ideas and theory on social phenomena to accommodate and explain the presence in and effects of software on the human world.

When thinking about the human understanding of the world and the role of software in that understanding in the "digital age," a computational dimension is inserted into the "given" (Berry, 2011: 141). That "given" implies that the ontology of the computational is increasingly hegemonic in forming the background presupposition for our understanding of the world. Our referential totality that is the world in a phenomenological sense is increasingly filled with actors enabled with computational techniques (Berry, 2011: 141). Screens and interfaces can be understood as a window onto this world and the keyboard and mouse operate as equipment with which we might manipulate it. While that manipulation is never direct, and the presence of vicarious causation is something that needs to be accounted for in understanding the software-mediated world (Harman, 2009; Berry, 2011), it does form a critical part of the way that humans navigate and understand the software-inflected and mediated world. The approach of treating software as a factor in understanding of the world avoids treating software as a mere commodity and is more akin to treating software as a thing. This means treating it "as a neighbourhood, as an amalgamation. It also means thinking through its simultaneous ambiguity and specificity" (Chun, 2011: 21). The field and challenge of software studies is therefore straightforward: to acknowledge software as a key factor in the social reality and lived-in experience of the world and to study code on these terms rather than as a functional assemblage to execute commands.

Software studies and spatiality

A criticism of some work in software studies is that there is a lack of attention to spatiality as a key consideration in the mediation of software in everyday life. As a factor in the world, software shapes societal relations and economic processes through the automatic production of space (Thrift and French, 2002) that generates new spatialities and the creation of software-sorted or machine-readable geographies that alter the nature of access and governance (how societies are organised and governed to fulfil certain aims) (Dodge and Kitchin, 2011: 7). Dodge and Kitchin argue that the effect of software (or code) on spatial understanding is to continually modify space; that is continually bring space into existence through processes of transduction that emerge from the functioning of code. Transduction in this instance refers to an operation in which a particular domain undergoes an ontogenetic modulation (Mackenzie, 2003: 10). Ontogenesis refers to a domain coming into existence (Dodge and Kitchin, 2004: 170). In practice the use of computational devices, as an extension of the rules and instructions of software (code), continually shapes the understanding of place through interactions with coded objects and technologies that bring spaces into existence (or awareness). Code acts as a catalyst for transduction and in particular as a catalyst for technicity, that is the effect of technology mediating, supplementing and augmenting everyday life (Dodge and Kitchin, 2004: 169). The effect of these transductions is to create a series of coded practices that are a combination of code and human practices that become a way of acting and being in the world, specifically in understanding and acting in spaces that undergo transductions. The understanding of space as code/space (Dodge and Kitchin, 2011) is an acknowledgement that some spaces are dependent on code to come into being as intended, and that a breakdown of that code can lead to space being alternatively modulated into a different state of being.

The presence of computation in everyday life is usually manifested through specific kinds of media that allow code to be executed. Coyne specifically investigates how digital devices influence the way people use spaces, and argues that such devices are mobile "tuning" devices in that they draw information into, and out of, situations to help users establish a sense of place (Coyne, 2010: 223). In this way, they "tune" the user to the place through the incremental changes that the device makes to the experience of place until an attunement to the place is achieved. As such, the computational device, and the code that it is dependent upon, is part of the user's attunement to the world. This attunement is part of the possibility of understanding place as place rather than geometric space through the practices of use that the user employs in using the device in everyday life, rather than the pervasive interjections from the device that Coyne (2010: 240) identifies as important in the device tuning the user to space. So, when one views the world with the assistance of computational devices, software or code (or "computationally", as Berry terms this) one is already comported towards the world in a way that assumes it has already been mapped, classified and digitised. Space and place are constructed through computational devices that offer this worldview back through a plethora of computational mediators, such as mobile phones, car navigation systems or handheld computers (Berry, 2011: 137).

Due to this dependence on media, a feature of code is that it relies on a notion of spatiality that is formed by the peculiar linear form of computer memory and the idea of address space (Berry, 2011: 111). As far as a computer is concerned, memory is a storage device that could be located anywhere in the world. Data is requested, it is processed, and then it is sent back to the memory. Code therefore easily fits within a network topology when addressing data, which explains why it can be so painstaking to model abstract space within the software, which may be spread over the globe. For example, the difference between two places, whether Sydney and Anchorage or Swansea and Cardiff, is equidistant in the topology of the network. Data may take longer to arrive between two geographical points but this does not necessarily indicate physical distance as the way in which data is transmitted follows paths that are not strictly efficient geographically. This is, of course, how the Internet is able to function as a topological, as opposed to physical, structure in software (Berry, 2011: 111). This spatiality creates a powerful way of combining systems from across the world into coherent systems for work, eradicating distance and time as barriers to interaction and opening possibilities for contact between machines and humans (in a software-mediated sense). The spatiality of software studies is therefore not only the space of human interaction with computational devices, but also the spaces that are opened through the functioning of code and the ability of networks to overcome geographic and temporal barriers.

More prosaically, ICTs have material effects on how cities and regions are configured, built and managed with the development of smart buildings, the networking of physical infrastructure, the use of information and control systems and so on. Batty (1997b: 155) termed this the computable city, noting that "planners ... are accustomed to using computers to advance our science and art but it would appear that the city itself is turning into a constellation of computers" (cited in Dodge and Kitchin, 2011: 18). Mackenzie (2010) develops a similar line of thinking in discussing the phenomenon of *wirelessness*, arguing that the continual engagement with computational devices and gadgets leads to a tendency to make network connections at all times in the current networked world. This tendency is an embodiment of an attunement to computational devices and gadgets that provide information to users and indicates an awareness of network connections as a fundamental part of living in a world with a proliferation of computational devices. Other pertinent insights come from Shepard (2011: 18) who argues that increasingly the "dataclouds of the 21st century" shape experience of the city, and Gordon and de Souza e Silva (2008, 2011) whose concept of *networked locality* emphasises how particular usage of networked devices and the information they can provide from de-localised storage can increase nearness to places rather than increase distance in a phenomenological sense. As a field of study, software studies must be concerned with the dual articulation of software on spatiality that is expressed in all these works: the physical configuration of cities, spaces and places and the ability to transcend the geographical and open new spaces of collaboration, labour, communication and contact through networks that are dependent on the functioning of code.

Given this requirement, research on LBSN that fits into this field has concentrated on the possibilities of opening up and creating new spatialities through the use of LBSN. Analyses of the impact of location-based services have been myriad in consideration, but some major areas of research have emerged. Wilken (2012: 243) identifies the major themes as research directed towards analysing how locative technologies mediate the relationship between technology use and physical or digital spaces (see Wilken, 2008, 2011; Crawford and Goggin, 2009; de Souza e Silva and Frith, 2010; de Souza e Silva and Sutko, 2011; Wilken and Goggin, 2012), discussions of power and politics in location-based services (see Elmer, 2010), and assessments and discussions on the nature of the representation of space that emerge through locative media (Gazzard, 2011). In addition, the area of privacy has been a major area of interest (See Michael and Michael, 2009; Friedland and Sommer, 2010; Mascetti et al., 2010).

Research does support the notion that mobile media itself alters the way that users relate to physical space in a confluence of location and digital networks that mediates geographic places (Campbell and Ling,

2008; Gordon et al., 2013; Martin, 2014: 180). The ubiquity of connectivity with mobile communications (Okazaki and Mendez, 2013), the perpetual contact with social ties and continual potential of accessibility of social ties that creates a continual co-presence (Ling and Horst, 2011) and the possibility of instant interactivity with others (Campbell and Kwak, 2011), are the features of mobile Internet use that create the possibility and affordance of a transformation of the experience of place when using mobile media. Gordon et al. (2013) argue that location-based services mediate conceptions of space and geography while contributing to changes in understandings of participation in public life for users. Sheller (2002: 39) argued that mobile computational usage necessitates a rethinking of the term "publics" in light of the re-conceptualisation and re-spatialisation that mobile communications are creating through allowing publics to be more "mobile". The general use of the technology does not detract from conversing with others in public space (Campbell and Kwak, 2011: 207) and indeed can lead to more interaction as major events are relayed in real time to users in the same location. Hampton et al. (2010: 701) found that online activities in public spaces may contribute to higher overall levels of social engagement than in spaces where Internet connectivity is not available. These social considerations are important as they indicate that sociability and *being-social* are concerns regarding the use of location-based media, but rather than a decrease in sociability, what is being affected by the use of services like LBSN is an alteration or mediation of social practices.

While critical, these studies of location-based services and mobile media do not engage directly with the key issue I am concerned with, which is how the possibility of the subjective experience of place is afforded (or not) through the use of mobile technology. The work of Larissa Hjorth (2011, 2012) is perhaps indicative of the kind of work that more directly relates to my concerns. Hjorth's two-year ethnography of mobile media users in Seoul concentrated on the renegotiation of privacy and place in light of mobile media use. She focused on the ways that users are grappling with locative media and how using applications to move through and navigate urban space is in a continual trade-off with being concerned about privacy. This is then further explored with reference to identity, place and community. Hjorth's work is clearly within the software studies approach: this is research that looks to understand the presence of software as a transformative agent in the lives of users and key to understanding the world, while being an object of concern and circumspection in the lives of actors. The means of uncovering this presence – ethnography using interviews, focus groups and participant observation – are methods that my own empirical research adopted.

Gordon and de Souza e Silva's (2011) pivotal work, *Net Locality*, assesses location-based services as technologies that open up hybrid realities between location and technology that require new ways of thinking about them in order to understand the radical changes underway. A hybrid situation in this view is one where the local and the remote cannot be clearly defined as the mobile technology pulls in remote information to inform the situated actor in the local context. The presence and more importantly use of this information in a local context has a transformative effect on the experience of space for the user: the presence of the software transforms place. This approach obviously resonates with the investigation that is the core of this book; while I focus on the subjective phenomenological experience of places for users of a particular kind of location-based service, Gordon and de Souza e Silva's work encompasses the critical feature of contextual information available in real-time, thanks to continuous connectivity.

Humphreys' (2005, 2008, 2010) work utilising ethnography is indicative as a model of the kind of research and depth of findings that are being attempted in the current studies. Humphreys argues that mobile phones provide a unique opportunity to examine how new media affects the social world. The research suggests people map their understanding of common social rules and dilemmas onto new technologies, and over time this creates a new social landscape. Humphreys (2008) extended these ideas to studying the LBSN Dodgeball concluding that the app can influence the way informants in the study experienced public space and the social relations therein, and that Dodgeball could facilitate the creation of "third spaces," which are dynamic and iterant forms of social places. Humphreys (2010) returns to these themes by arguing that mobile social networking has the potential to transform the ways that people come together and interact in public space and will allow new kinds of information to flow into public spaces. This research is important in understanding the effects of LBSN on the relationship between place and user. I investigate the same kind of technology usage as investigated by Humphreys, albeit from a different philosophical perspective.

The experience of place and computationally-infused world are two critical aspects of the theory I forward in the following chapters. The mode of being in the world is also critical too; embodiment and the presence of the body in space demands consideration. Embodied interaction is a concept which centres around "the creation, manipulation and sharing of meaning through engaged interaction with artefacts" (Dourish, 2001). In LBSN, tangible computing is allied to social computing (social networking) and location services embedded in tangible devices, with the use of these devices resulting in the production of an embodied agent: intelligent agents that interact with the environment through a physical or virtual body. This model is illustrative of the approach to embodiment in this work. Bilandzic and Foth (2012) have reviewed research into locative media, mobile technology and embodied spatial interaction and suggest that research using experience design is ideal for investigating phenomenological hypotheses and questions. While the study of user experience implies a focus on the relationship between the user and a particular artefact, experience design focuses on the needs, emotions and meanings of people's everyday experiences. They suggest focusing on situated experiential aspects of use (cf. Millard and Soylu, 2009), which is an approach I adopted in my empirical research (rather than materialistic aspects of a specific artefact (cf. Dourish, 2001)).

The work of Farman (2012) is an example of a phenomenological approach where the relationship between user and mobile computational device is understood through the prism of embedded cognition where embodiment and space are co-constitutive; and mobile computational devices are entities that can reconfigure the way that users can embody that space of which they are co-constitutive. This Merleau-Ponty-influenced approach positions the user as an active part of the mediation of the world with (as opposed to by) the medium, and it is this consideration of the contribution of the individual as a meaningful entity in the process of mediation that I develop further. Farman's notions of the "sensory inscribed body" positions embodiment as critical to the usage of mobile media and gives the body a critical role in the effects of mobile media. The body itself is seen in this approach as the necessary vehicle for being in the world, and space is always constructed simultaneously with embodiment in that space (2012: 18). This embodiment is therefore relational and the notion of tuning in and out of different parts of the world (2012: 27) is a kernel of the view of placehood. Full embodied presence in this view is always deferred; we are always to a lesser or greater extent embodying space. Most importantly, Farman confirms the line of thinking that mobile technologies are reconfiguring the ways in which users can embody space and locate themselves in digital and virtual spaces simultaneously.

Farman's acknowledgement of phenomenology and embodiment has influenced my own thinking greatly, but nonetheless we differ with respect to the importance attached to subjectivity and phenomenological presence and its influence on place. While Farman concentrates on embodiment as key to understanding spatiality, I look to phenomenological mood and orientation. As Frith (2012) puts it, location-based services give the possibility of a personal database city where the subjective experience of places is both coded into databases and fed back to users, making the device and location-based service a critical aspect of the subjective experience of place. Embodiment plays a critical role in this theoretical account, but embodiment is positioned as a means of accessing information in the taken-for-granted processes and behaviours of using mobile devices. While accepting that we are always embodied in space, space and place are differentiated through the mood of the user of devices. Therefore, I explore the subjective experience of place as a distinct phenomenological category of being-in-the-world. This is not done through introspection alone; embodiment and a view of the data-infused environment are necessary to understand how the mood of the user towards technology and location is critical in the phenomenological understanding of place that arises from usage of mobile technology. What is being proposed is in essence a *post-Heideggerian phenomenology* or a *digital post-phenomenology of place*, where mood or orientation, embodied practices and the data-infused environment are co-constitutive of place.

In order to explore this *digital post-phenomenology of place* created in conjunction with computational devices, in Chapter 2, LBSN is considered as part of a historical movement in mapping. The chapter details the development of mapping techniques over time and seeks to understand how these changes in mapping have reflected changes in the dominant modes of understanding the world over history, from pre-modern understanding, to modernism, and to the computational understanding of the world involving the integration of social and semantic gazetteers in social mapping and location-based social networking that are becoming a part of a computational way of navigating the everyday world.

Chapter 3 begins the development of a phenomenology of place. Heidegger's account of the history of the understanding of being and spatiality in *Being and Time* (1962) is used to understand how the computational device can be used in a manner that allows for a "deep" or meaningful revealing of place. Following this, the use of care as a means to understand the relationship between user and thing in the world is elaborated. This is followed by a discussion of technology in Heidegger's "The Question Concerning Technology" (1977) as a means of understanding the way in which the space created by bringing things into care is annihilated by technicity. In arguing how this technological mode of revealing can be avoided in using geo-locational technology, the importance of the care structure and attunement with things is linked to the ideas of dwelling and the Thing found in Heidegger's works, "Building, Thinking, Dwelling" (2008) and "The Thing" (2008). Dwelling (and therefore thinking in the phenomenological sense) is proposed as contingent upon care and the attunement of Dasein to things. The chapter provides a framework for understanding spatiality through considering the attunement of Dasein, the practices involved with using geo-locative devices and applications, and the world-revealing that comes forth from this relationship between thing, user and environment.

Chapter 4 positions the computational device as a "thing" through a discussion of the materiality of the device and how the components and construction of the smartphone can comport the user towards the world in a manner that allows for a revealing of place. This analysis of the materiality of the device is linked to the embodiment of using smartphones and other devices and the presence of code and digital infrastructures around the user as an enabler of connection with other users in a phenomenological as well as digital sense. This furthers the Heideggerian phenomenology into a post-phenomenology that encapsulates the body and the computational milieu of the world filled with computational devices. The practices of embodied interaction involved are exemplified through an analysis of the Foursquare check-in code. The role of code and computation is conceptualised in this analysis of LBSN through an engagement with Peter Sloterdijk's theory of spheres. Code and computation are positioned as the enablers of the social in LBSN use, as the ability to connect with and understand place through connections with other users. Here, the social in coded spaces – spaces that are augmented or afford the possibility of connectivity through digital media (Dodge and Kitchin, 2011: 17–18) – is explained as "foam" that contributes to a *digital post-phenomenology of place* along with the situatedness and attunement of the user to the place through the embodied use of LBSN. Foam is described by Sloterdijk as a spatial constitution that acts as a meta-collector that accumulates spaces of assembly and non-assembly (Sloterdijk, 2004). In this conceptual spatial assemblage, people experience assembly and communication as they move from bubble (Sloterdijk's term for dyadic communicative linkages between entities) to bubble. In the computationally-infused environment, as is well documented elsewhere, this is aided and abetted by the use of social media. Social media and location-based social media are part of the computational milieu and everyday life experience of users of this technology, and the continual assembly and dissolution of bubbles and spheres of experience in the foam is enabled through the use of computational devices and applications. This positions the critical computational elements of LBSN (code, data, interface, function) as facilitators in communication and provision of information that allow for a feeling of placehood to arise as people make meaningful connections with others and the social gazetteers that are provided by LBSN.

Chapter 5 applies this post-phenomenology of digital devices through an investigation of ethnographic research undertaken with Foursquare users. The purpose of this is to assess and contextualise, theoretically, responses, practices of use and behaviour that are indicative of using LBSN to reveal and understand place in a non-technological sense. Usage of LBSN that allows users to explore the world, navigate novel places and gain an understanding of places as meaningful will be linked to the theoretical discussion in Chapters 3 and 4. Chapter 6 examines the practices and orientation to the world that are indicative of a technological revealing of space through LBSN usage. This chapter draws upon the account of technology in "The Question Concerning Technology" to illustrate how particular usages of LBSN taken from the ethnography of users can be indicative of a technological understanding of place and how this is related to a particular orientation to device and world that does not allow for the taking into care of the device. This is in contrast to understandings of place analysed in Chapter 5.

Finally, Chapter 7 summarises the efficacy of digital post-phenomenology. The methodological issues the study raises are also discussed, in particular the issues that come from trying to collect empirical data for a phenomenological study. The book concludes with a brief discussion of the future of LBSN and digital devices in light of the findings of this research.

2
A (Brief) History of Understanding Space and Place

The primary consideration of this chapter is how maps and other location technologies are representations of how humans have considered territory over time, and as such a reflection of how place has been understood over time. The purpose of this chapter is to offer a selective outline of the historical development of mapping systems and technologies from early ancient maps of the pre-Socratic Greek era to the development of Ordnance Survey maps in Great Britain, Global Positioning System technology and databases of places. In doing this, the stages of cartography are contrasted and paralleled with dominant expressions and forms of knowledge and understanding of the world that dominated both formal and lay epistemology at those times. As such, the map and technique of mapping becomes an extension of (although not a causal extension) of forms of knowledge that are dominant at a particular time – a cartographic *biopower*, to borrow from Foucault, referring to the regulation of subjects through mapping techniques. These changes over time are articulated in the aims and objectives of mapping projects, in the scope of the maps proposed and in the methods used to create maps, from military organised programmes to the open digital mapping and crowdsourced mapping that occurs today with location-based social networking.

The clearest theoretical links for understanding how maps and ways of knowing the world change over time are from Michel Foucault's genealogical accounts of the emergence of the subject. Foucault places the discussion of a subject in the context of the emergence of disciplines, control, and power. Foucault also identifies discourse as the mechanism by which power relations are expressed and structured. Here, how subjectification leaves the individual prone to control is of great interest. Foucault (most clearly in *Discipline and Punish*) argues modernity has produced power structures that organise and structure individuals and that these power structures exist to order and control all life, not just beings that are involved in the creation of these power structures. In this sense, modern power – exemplified by Foucault in examples like Bentham's panopticon from *Discipline and Punish* – exists to create docile bodies and self-absorbed subjects for the aim of greater welfare for all (Dreyfus, 2004). The result of these practices Foucault termed "disciplinary bio-power" (Foucault, 1995: 191) and Foucault sees that the practices of power are grounded in research and sciences, or disciplines.

The aim of the disciplines (and we can take cartography as a discipline in the sense Foucault used the term here) is, therefore, to identify an anomaly (e.g. delinquency), to bring the anomaly under the disciplines of research (such as Geography) and to normalise the anomaly. The totalising tendency of disciplinary power is exhibited in dominant discourses. In the context of mapping, we can understand the examples that are used in this chapter as forms of disciplinary power, both in the way that the representation of place orients and controls concepts of place for the subject (or user) and how the form and method of representation is an extension of power structures in modern society. Implicitly, then, LBSN is positioned as a cartographic method of representing place that is indicative of a shift in both thinking about and being disciplined to think about place, and the role of the ethnography and analysis is to uncover what this altered relationship to place is in practice for users of the technology. Prior to that, though, it is useful to try and understand how power and power relations have been expressed in cartographic methods previously.

As was explained in the Introduction, I propose a post-Heideggerian post-phenomenological approach to understand how LBSN has had a transformative effect on the understanding of place for users. The critique of technology from Martin Heidegger will play a major role, but at this point it is also useful to utilise some observations on Heidegger's philosophy to flesh out the idea of different cartographic techniques and methods that may be indicative of dominant modes of thinking about the world (and in particular place). Dreyfus (1989: 97) argues that Heidegger offers six epochs of being that can be understood as onto-theological shifts in understanding of being, and these can be understood as different dominant ways of conceptualising, explaining and understanding the world. The first major epoch identified was (i) *Physis* or coming-forth, where things and beings emerge of their own volition without intervention from humans. The first major shift is to *Poesis*: a letting-come-forth where humans allows things to take shape through craft (for example, a craftsman allows the coming forth of the chalice from silver). (ii) *Techne* furthers this, into a bringing-forth where the craftsman no longer responds to the material, but instead shapes for the needs of the community. This corresponds to Plato's covering up of the clearing with metaphysics – the material as a thing is no longer considered as a thing, but instead its materiality must correspond to a form to be created or brought forth that is more perfect than the material as thing itself. This progressed to (iii) *Res*, a produced-forth from the Roman understanding of things as finished works rather than materials brought together, or of the processes and raw materials being things in themselves. During the pre-enlightenment domination of Catholicism in Europe, a (iv) *Ens creatum* or the medieval understanding of being as the notion of a master creator as the responsible for being. The age of modernity emerged as a (v) subject-centred understanding of being, beginning with Descartes' introduction of representation of the world, in Kant's notion of *Vorstellung*. Being is understood as that which can represent the world and set forth (Man).

This final epoch is the modern world of (vi) technological revealing, where humans represent all things (through the subject-object distinction that is an ontotheology) by bringing "what is present to hand before oneself as something standing over against, to relate it to oneself, to the force representing it and to force it back into this relationship with oneself as the normative realm" (Heidegger, 1977: 131). Being is understood as the thing that stands in relation to all other things as objects, not as things with essences or meanings (i.e. "things" rather than objects) beyond being a resource to be used. Heidegger (1977: 153) argued the totalising effect of the technological understanding of being could erase humans, a view shared by Foucault in his understanding of bio-power, and that post-humanism would not be a liberating development in the history of human beings.

From this, there are two important points to be taken forward. As Heidegger states, history is not a sequence of events, but consists of the "goals of creative activity, their rank and their extent" and this pursuing of goals following historical ontotheologies forms the subject matter for historical reflection (Heidegger, 1994: 36). Secondly, ontotheology or metaphysics, that is the dominant mode of understanding being in a particular epoch or age, acts to order and orient us towards understanding the world itself. An ontotheology necessarily re-orders any understanding of being in line with the mode of understanding in that ontotheology – in late modernity, we are oriented to understand the world (and those things in that "world," which would of course include places) as a realm of resources to be used in the achieving of human aims. This will consequently affect the understanding of place and should be a facet of an analysis of cartographic forms – if the historical analysis of being presented here is accurate. While the remainder of this chapter in no way presupposes to be an exhaustive history of cartography or cartographic thought, the examples selected here are for the purpose of illustration of a movement through these stages of understanding the world in a particular way that moves towards a technological understanding of place and is then subverted by the social and user-generated aspects of LBSN and crowdsourced cartography.

Historical maps as a letting-come-forth

A history of mapping that corresponds with a history of being or an analysis of dominant modes of knowledge and understanding can begin with pre-Socratic mapping, as this is a form of map that illustrates nicely the notion of a letting-come-forth of the territory as an understanding of place. One obvious problem is the lack of actual maps from this ancient time, and the relatively undeveloped art of cartography at the time.[1] To address what such a form of knowing about the world may be like with regard to place, Heidegger's analysis of the temple in "The Origin of the Work of Art" (2008) can be read as a way of understanding the role of a *thing* (the Temple) in creating a place. Heidegger (2008: 168–179) describes the Greek temple as a thing that takes what is initially inchoate and is withdrawn i.e. in the background of the world, and gathers it into a world-defining thing (Guignon, 2004: 404). It is the temple that, when built, lets the valley and the surrounding environment take a determinate form that stands in relation to the temple and has meaning in reference to the temple as a thing (Guignon, 2004: 401).

> It is the temple-work that first fits together and at the same time gathers around itself the unity of those paths and relations in which birth and death, disaster and blessing, victory and disgrace, endurance and decline acquire the shape (Gestalt) of destiny (Geschick) for human being. (Heidegger, 1971: 42)

The temple is a thing that performs work in the world, and the nature of that work is both to provide meaning (or shape) to human experience and from that, to guide experience after the work-event – a work of art. The nature of this work is a revealing: the temple allows the environment to be revealed as a letting-come-forth in that it does not bring-forth intentionally, but allows for the environment to become meaningful and part of the circumspection of human being through its work in the world. Guignon describes this as how the world-defining[2] work of art responds to and takes up a primal strife of concealing and unconcealing and defines that strife in a way that keeps it a question in the world not concealed by ontotheology (Guignon, 2004: 401). Heidegger's understanding of the temple is as a *thing* that lets *things come forth* by gathering them within a referential totality, and therefore spatiality must be understood as how things stand in relation to one another and how this standing in relation to one another allows being to become intelligible to Dasein.

This appears tangential to a discussion of mapping, but it is relevant as this kind of understanding of geographical features as things that create places is central to an understanding of place as revealed poetically. A poetic revealing of place is a revealing where "things" are revealed as having essences other than just resources to be used, while a technological revealing reveals all things as resources to be used; space as something endlessly divisible, fixed and understood mathematically. In the example of the Greek temple, the work of the temple is as world-revealing, gathering what was previously withdrawn and making it intelligible through this gathering-forth. This work is not intentional on the part of the architect, labourer or worshiper; it is done as the thing (the temple) "things" in gathering forth the elements of the world and revealing the world as such. In doing this, the revealing is a *poesis*, or poetic revealing of place; revealing that is unforced, allowing the elements of the world to come forth. In the example of the temple, while the temple has clearly been designed and built for a purpose, that purpose is worship rather than bringing forth the environment. In the example Heidegger gives, the letting-come-forth work of the temple is just that, a letting become unconcealed features of the world that were previously withdrawn from circumspection.

Secondly, this understanding allows for an anticipation of what a poetic revealing of location by a map may be like. The map is a representation of the territory, and as such is susceptible to Radloff's (2007: 44) critique that "the representational dimension ... dissolves the site into the uniformity of the planetary dimension" with the planetary dimension referring to the understanding of territory through scientific means. The particular Gestalt of such a representation is therefore as a resource to be used or a technological revealing of location. This view of the representation derives from the scientific worldview that is based on and reinforces the subject-object distinction that Heidegger identified as indicative of the modern understanding of being, and Foucault identifies as bio-power. Maps that represent the world as an object to the subject that is the person are the focus of such an analysis, and as such a map involved with a poetic revealing of the world would reveal in another way. The argument here is that such a map would be one that reveals the world not from "a view from nowhere" (Nagel, 1986) but one where the world is understood as a system of co-referential entities in the manner that Heidegger's temple does its world-revealing work.

An example of this kind of map is Anaximander's map of the world. Anaximander lived between 610 and 546 BCE and is credited with having created one of the first maps of the world. In Anaximander's map the world is seen as circular in form, with the known lands of the world (parts of Europe, North Africa and Western Asia) grouped around the Aegean Sea in the centre. This pre-Socratic map shows the world as what is known; all things stand in reference to the Aegean Sea, and only those things that are significant are mapped. The centrality of the most relevant and most known – and the point of subjective position – to the map is critical, as all things sit *in relation to the point at which the cartographer (and indeed civilisation as was known at the time to the Greeks) was situated*, and the surrounding territory as known is relational to that centre.

This map is a map of the (known) world from the time, but is also a *local* map, in that it holds all those places and territories in relation to that which is local and near, rather than a map that flattens territory (in that all places and spaces are afforded the same importance via scale, ignoring the subjective importance of place). This is a kind of revealing of place that is subjective and does not reduce place to resource.

The Ordnance Survey

In contrast, the Ordnance Survey (OS) is an example of mapping from the modern epoch of the history of being – that is that the map is a representation of the territory it purports to represent. Maps of this kind represent only physical characteristics of the territory and significant buildings or landmarks through the use of gazetteers that symbolise those man-made constructions. The OS is an executive agency of the United Kingdom Government, responsible for the mapping of Great Britain and Northern Ireland and the production of maps. The agency originated from the Board of Ordnance, an arm of the British military that was responsible for the supply of armaments and munitions to the Army until 1830, and which was also responsible for the production and distribution of maps for military purpose (Oliver, 2005: 10).

The OS began as an exercise in the production of military intelligence, specifically in 1747 when Lieutenant-Colonel David Watson requested the production of a map of the Scottish Highlands to assist in the subjection of the clans, following the Jacobite rising of 1745. In response to this request, King George II commissioned a military survey of the Highlands, under the command of the Duke of Cumberland and assisted by an engineer, William Roy. Roy's work in particular resulted in "The Duke of Cumberland's Map" (Oliver, 2005: 10). Roy would later (in 1763, 1766 and 1783) make proposals for an official survey of the whole of Britain, based on the original work in the Highlands. The impetus to construct these maps of enemy territory was obvious: military aims and requirements and the need for accurate surveys of enemy territory to effectively attack that territory. The explicit use of the maps produced by the OS for military, economic and political understanding of territory points to the development of the technological mode of understanding being, and is illustrative of the shift in ontotheology to modernity.

The beginning in earnest of the OS is considered to be 1783, when the Royal Societies of Paris and London decided to end their long-running dispute as to the relative positions of astronomical observatories in those two cities (Oliver, 2005: 9). This dispute was resolved through applying the process of triangulation to the two observatories (Seymour, 1980: 6).[3] Although ostensibly a civil project, the leadership of a major-general in the project (assisted in completion by the Royal Artillery) still indicates a military interest in the production of maps for military advantage; the use of mapping to settle a political dispute is also significant, and indicates the importance that mapping technology and map production would have in the political process in the future. The advent of war with France in 1793 provided a further stimulus to the mapping of the UK in an accurate and rapid manner in the context of defence. In 1795, the decision had been taken to survey the entire country to publish a collection of accurate maps of considerable strategic value in defending the country militarily (Oliver, 2005: 12).[4] A new development was the publication for public consumption of the surveys. This was initially in response to requests from landowners in the counties that had been surveyed, but an unintentional consequence of this was to create a public demand for OS maps, evidenced by purchases of maps of Lincolnshire by non-landowners (Oliver, 2005: 13). This development is the first instance of a commercial element to the work of the OS.

By 1870, the OS had passed from military to civilian control through government, though it remained organised on military lines (Oliver, 2005: 15). In 1890, the OS was transferred to the Board of Agriculture, reflecting the importance of OS maps in land ownership establishment and issues (Seymour, 1980). The department set out regulations for the regular revision of maps on the established scales, with no 1:25,000 scale map allowed to be more than 20 years out of date. World War I and the enlisting of both military and civilian members of the OS delayed large-scale revisions, and these delays were exacerbated by post-war economic conditions. By 1939 and the outbreak of World War II, progress had been made in cutting down the arrears in revisions, and the development of National Grid mapping had began (Oliver, 2005: 17). The recasting of OS maps on metric grid sheets would continue until the early 1980s, and would go hand in hand with the transfer of scales from imperial to metric units, with the metrication programme beginning in 1969; maps were produced in 1cm:10,000cm and 1cm:50,000cm units (Oliver, 2005: 15).

With metrification and the completion of the national grid resurvey, in 1978 an Ordnance Survey Review Committee was appointed to determine and define the core activities of the OS. Those activities defined as core would be eligible for grants from the Exchequer, and all other activities had to be funded on a commercial basis (Oliver, 2005: 20). A practical result of this was that the pricing of individual maps changed to reflect the need to recover drawing and surveying costs no longer covered by the Exchequer, and by the late 1990s around 90% of these costs were being recovered through sales of maps (Oliver, 2005: 20).[5] The movement of the OS map from military tool to economic and political tool to commercial artefact could now been seen as complete.

The digitisation of the maps produced by the OS began in small-scale experiments in 1969, but problems with producing satisfactory small-scale maps from large databases hindered early work (Oliver, 2005: 18). Through increased investment and prioritisation of digitisation in the 1980s, the digitising programme was completed in 1995, and increasingly OS data is now provided in digital form. In 2001 the OS launched a project that established a seamless information base that underpins a new generation of detailed, digital master maps called OSMasterMap (Oliver, 2005: 19). This geospatial database allows for multiple levels of data – that is, data on places, events, photos, descriptions, videos and other media forms – to be ingratiated into the OS map architecture, or to be linked to OS maps. Data from OSMasterMap now offers up to date referencing on 440 million man-made and natural landscapes in the UK. From 2 April 2010, OS maps were made freely available for the first time directly from the OS via digital downloads, marking a radical departure from the previous finance model but in line with demands for free and open data, led by Sir Tim Berners-Lee, and from within the outgoing Labour government (Arthur, 2010). The OSOpenData initiative was expected to cost around £20 million in forgone revenues, with the difference funded by the Treasury (Arthur, 2010). This change in policy reflects the ease of access to alternative forms of map for the UK, such as the Google Earth programme, freely available as a download on multiple platforms from Google, or Openstreetmap, a user-generated content-based mapping service built by users. The change to free access is part of an attempt to preserve the relevance of OS at a time when its viability is questionable due to the proliferation of free alternatives, while preserving the brand of the OS as a platform for future data-driven economic innovation.

The history of the OS shows cartography as a top-down activity (Crampton, 2009: 1). Persons in positions of political and military power created maps, and primarily the history of the OS is one of military and political power. The military origins of the organisation, and the function of the maps produced to serve that function is clear. The political significance of the OS is also clear, from the early engagements with mapping for political needs to the absorption of the organisation by the civil government and its subsequent involvement in matters of taxation and state revenue. Moreover, the production of maps became a means of funding the OS in itself, a purely economic turn away from the political economic functioning of the OS under military and civilian governance. People that produce maps are affected by the ideological and cultural influences placed upon them in their role as cartographers in society, and as such, there emerges a need to acknowledge that maps as products and artefacts generate specific territorial knowledge or what Olsson (2007) calls cartographic reason. Cartographic reason can be linked to Foucault's notion of bio-politics (Foucault, 1998: 140) and the political production of knowledge. The state plays a fundamental role in production of maps, as can be seen from the history of the OS. The top-down position of cartographers and the OS, as functionaries within government itself, allows the maps produced to be seen as products of the state which exist to normalise concepts of territory and space for those subjects under the power of a particular state, normalising power relations within the state (for example, through the establishment and clarification between the boundaries of unitary authorities in the United Kingdom). Foucault's notion of bio-politics has parallels with Heidegger's technological epoch of the understanding of being (Dreyfus, 2004); bio-politics refers to the style of government that regulates populations through bio-power, or the application of political power on human life and can therefore be understood as a means of organising and ordering. The technological understanding of being can also be understood as an ordering (Malpas, 2008: 289), in that the kind of revealing that emerges from a technological understanding of being is a revealing of all things as resource, a mode of ordering as resource.

This technological kind of ordering is essentially tied to the measurable and the calculable (Malpas, 2008: 282), whereas the ordering of equipment (such as the Temple) is an ordering that is a "towards-which" or "in-order-to" (Malpas, 2008: 134). The OS map, in revealing location in a technological mode of revealing, allows for entities to only appear insofar as they are available to this ordering as resource, as something that is held in reserve to be used. The metaphysical disclosure of the thing as a worlding presence, as seen in the example of the temple, gives way to this ordering (Malpas, 2008: 282). In the historical development of the OS, one observes that the creation of maps goes through a series of orderings that satisfy needs for resource – the military need, the economic need, the political need, the commercial need – that have the effect of organising the representation of location as a means to satisfy such needs as resource. This kind of technological ordering of the world acts through a certain form of spatial thinking about the world and all things in it, of which the OS map acts as a representation. Place in the technological mode of revealing shows up as nothing more than spatial "position" or iconography, meaning, for Malpas, that place does not show up at all, but instead is only the co-ordinate of space with things only appearing as "nodes within a uniform spatial array" (Malpas, 2008: 293).

Malpas' characterisation of the technological revealing of place can be easily related to the conceptions of space of Descartes and Newton in the introduction. The technological mode of revealing reveals space as an empty, characterless series of homogenous regions which can be viewed as resource, along with anything found in those regions, mere spatial markers. The Cartesian concept of space – recall that space is only extension, and while the body is part of that extension it is of secondary importance to the intellect – relates closely to this understanding of space and place. Descartes argued that extension is perceived but is not understood through perception; understanding emerges from the operation of the intellect through the deduction of mathematical truths about space. The Cartesian understanding of space is as something exterior to the human being (we are in a subject-object relationship with space, and are necessarily separate from it) to be viewed in a systematic and calculating manner. This can be seen as akin to Malpas' (and of course Heidegger's) view of the technological revealing of space as revealing space as something calculable and measurable. The reduction of things to resource is the most significant aspect of this revealing.

Global Positioning Systems

Global Positioning Systems (GPS) technology locates an individual or object within the range of the technology by pinpointing their position on Earth through communication between a GPS-enabled device and a network of 24 satellites known as the Global Positioning System (Nelson, 1999). GPS represents a different paradigm in locational representation, no longer only graphical, but now precise and relational to other entities based on the spatial co-ordinates of latitude, longitude and altitude which GPS technology uses to locate the device or individual.

The history of GPS can be traced to methods of navigation used for centuries. Ostensibly, when navigators used angular measurements of celestial bodies to ascertain the position of a ship on the oceans, this was a primitive and relatively technologically unsophisticated method of determining the physical location of a ship (Nelson, 1999). The ability to pinpoint the location of a ship is an issue of safety but the commercial need for accuracy of positioning is also important in regard to the delivery of goods and the safety of cargo. The military need for greater precision in locational knowledge would increase as wars increased in scale from the 18th century to the 20th century, and particularly with the advent of submarine technology and the importance of the submarine as military equipment through the Second World War and the Cold War.

Transit, the US Navy Navigation Satellite System, was conceived in the late 1950s, and launched in the 1960s to provide accurate navigation data for Polaris missile submarines (Goebel, 2002).[6] If the orbit of a satellite was known, then a radio receiver's position could also be known relative to the orbit of that satellite (Goebel, 2002). The Transit system utilised this observation, the system comprising six satellites in circular, polar orbits at an altitude of 1,075km, with a period of revolution of 107 minutes. The orbits of the satellites were precisely determined by tracking them at widely distributed sites, and under favourable conditions the accuracy of measurements was within 35 to 100 metres. The Transit system was successful, but due to the large gaps in coverage in the system (as a result of the limited number of satellites and the positioning of those satellites) the application of the Transit system was constrained by security issues (Goebel, 2002).

The relative success of the Transit system led to a desire to improve the accuracy and utility of the system. The US Navy and US Air Force launched a joint programme in 1973 that would create the NAVSTAR Global Positioning System (Nelson, 1999). In contrast to Transit, NAVSTAR provides continuous coverage through utilising two kinds of observed measurements. The pseudo-range is calculated by observing the offset between a pseudorandom noise (PRN) coded signal from the satellite and a replica code generated by the user's device (Goebel, 2002). These methods of determining position are a form of triangulation between the user and four or more satellites, and the ranges are inferred from the time differentials of the satellites (Rip and Hasik, 2002: 65). The high precision of the positioning co-ordinates is made possible through the use of atomic clocks on the satellites – the precision of these clocks permitting real-time measurements of distance within a few metres (Parkinson and Spilker, 1996: 165; Goebel, 2002).[7] This continuation of the role of the military in GPS is important; despite the increasing commercial and civilian use of GPS, the system remains within the control and maintenance of the US military, and is used extensively for military purposes.

The achievements of the military application of GPS are significant, but the system has come to popular prominence through the use of GPS in the civilian and commercial realms. GPS has been used on large ships since the 1980s, for accurate navigation, but has received far more attention in its use in automobiles, known in that context as automotive navigation systems (ANS), mostly called SatNavs. ANSs use GPS navigation devices to acquire position data and to locate the user on a road in the unit's map database. Early GPS signals were available to civilian receivers, but the quality and frequency of signals were variable and often poor.[8] Magellan made the first ANS for cars in the US market in 1995, but the prohibitive cost and poor signal did not lead to large unit sales (Magellan, 2009). There was more commercial success in Japan, with Mitsubishi and Pioneer both launching systems in 1990, and a number of manufacturers such as Honda making GPS systems available in top-of-the-range models as integrated, rather than stand-alone, systems (Honda, 2009; Mitsubishi, 2010; Pioneer, 2010). ANSs typically have a visual and auditory interface consisting of a top-view for the map, numbers for distance, schematic pictograms and voice prompts for directions to specific addresses that match to entries in the unit database. The databases of places in these units have largely been proprietary, and have involved interesting economic developments like the ANS developer TomTom buying Tele Atlas, the digital map maker, for €2.9 billion in 2008 (Kloet, 2007). Apple's iPhone allows for the downloading of satellite navigation systems through their application store at a fraction of the price of a dedicated unit, and the availability and cost of applications for smartphones is affecting the market for ANS-dedicated devices.

GPS technology had its developmental roots in, and is still dependent upon, military technology. Until there is a realistic commercially developed and launched alternative to the NAVSTAR system, the US military will still be responsible for a technology that is now increasingly prevalent in the civilian realm, and for which there are major commercial implications. The development of GPS has obvious parallels with the OS: a military beginning rooted in defence and the need for superior information on location, followed by political intervention and a political economy based on the utilisation of the product in commercial markets and applications. Again, there is clear influence on the genealogical development of this technology from military, political and commercial forces that have led to the current proliferation of GPS-enabled devices.

In some ways, GPS is like a map in that it is a tool for location; however, the method of *locating* makes GPS a very different case. In operating a GPS device, the user is actively locating themselves in the world in relation to other objects, persons and landmarks as defined in databases. The means of locating – through communication with a satellite that triangulates the location of the user – marks the process as one of active de-territorialisation at a place that is located within a space defined through a database held by the device. In doing this, the device becomes an extension of the user (McLuhan, 2008: 8) but the location revealed by the use of GPS-utilising applications and systems is not a consideration of the territory as the spatial relations between gazetteers. As Coyne (2010: 152) argues, GPS is a highly technological response to the desire to orient to location, with none of the human processes of placing, positioning, naming or tagging involved. This amplifies the sense of an independent reality of space from humans (Coyne, 2010: 152), and the hegemony of GPS becomes a normalisation of that relationship. GPS as a means of location flattens all place to space, and the understanding of place is usurped by recognition of location as pure co-ordinate. This kind of mapping is closest to the Cartesian notion of space as both apart from the intellect and as matter only, endlessly divisible and quantifiable with no inherent meaning; meaning being provided only by the independent, rational observer who makes sense of the space. This is a technological realisation of the understanding of location as pure data to be shared and used as data.

Database of places

The development of GPS (and in particular the development of commercial applications of GPS for the civilian market) has led to a new kind of information source on location, which has developed directly from innovations in commercial GPS devices. GPS devices like ANSs require a database of places and geographical features to operate a functional user interface and it is this database that is the next development in locational technology. The databases used in GPS devices are proprietary ones, owned and controlled by the hardware manufacturers, or created by software companies and licensed by the hardware manufacturer. Either way, the system is closed; the user cannot alter the software or more importantly add to the software – proprietary Geographic Information Systems (GIS) are expensive to set up as software, and without extensive preparation this software can also be highly inaccurate – as many Apple users found out when updating to the iOS6 operating system for their mobile devices on 19 September 2012, to discover that the Google maps application had been replaced with Apple's own maps application. The new application, built on Openstreetmap, brought much derision due to its curious inaccuracies, such as labelling Berlin as "Schöneiche" (Butcher, 2012).

This kind of closed system can be contrasted to software programmes like Openstreetmap, which allow user-created content to build layers of information into maps and locational software, and is also in opposition to a series of user-created databases that are the product of interactive geospatial tagging applications for mobile platforms such as the iPhone. These applications, or location-based social networks (LBSNs) – Foursquare for example – build databases of places by users creating "spots" and "checking-in" at those spots. Foursquare launched on 13 March 2009, and had 50 million registered users by May 2014 (Foursquare, 2014). On Foursquare, users were (prior to an application redesign in August 2014) rewarded in points-based systems for the creation of and checking-in to spots, and from this a game environment is created where users are encouraged to compete with friends for high scores over periods of time. Users were also rewarded with badges and titles for check-ins and creating spots: Foursquare conveyed the status of "mayor" on users who had the most check-ins at a spot. Users can still leave comments about spots they check-in at (and as many of these spots are services like restaurants or shops, this can be seen as a form of free advertising or user-review of the service) and photographs of the place. Links with other social networks, with Facebook and Twitter being ubiquitous options, helps to find friends and to post real-time updates to potentially larger audiences – all while promoting the application itself across other platforms. By checking-in to a place, a list of nearby venues and places is automatically generated, providing the user with further information on their location and their relative position to other places and services. The database of places is built using user-generated content (be that geo-tagged places, comments or recommendations) and as such the database grows and develops as a function of the use of the LBSN.[9]

While the use of game design and gamification of location to attract and maintain users is interesting in these applications, it is the result of user activity that is more important. Usage creates a user-created database of places, which is aided by other content, such as comments and photos, that adds a social dimension to the database. The development of the database of places requires an understanding of the development of the technological and computational elements that contribute to its realisation. A user activates the application, which locates the user using GPS triangulation. This triangulated position is then matched up to spots that have been created nearby, for example a shop or restaurant. The users can check-in to this place (and leave a comment, and link this check-in to another social network) or if they are in another place nearby, can create a new spot. The spots are superimposed on a base map to insure accuracy,[10] but it is left to the user to check for the accuracy of their spot. Once created, other users can also check-in at this spot, and information on check-ins will be relayed to friends of the user through a message to their mobile device.

This shift in production is significant; in a top-down system the database is a created, closed interface, without the facility for user contribution or editing. In a bottom-up system, the users of the application create the information held in the database. This open form of database is contingent on users: some areas can be expected to have many spots, others none based on the relative facilities available and technological limitations (such as 3G coverage). These databases are also developing in isolation to one another as it can be expected that the more users an application has, the more potentially valuable to advertisers a database will become.[11] In this sense, the device and LBSN is not only a kind of media, but also a form of "me-dia" (Merrin, 2014) where the device focuses upon the individual in a hyper-localised manner, providing and producing specific and hyper-relevant information as a form of horizontal, peer-to-peer, mediated interpersonal communication.

Businesses do not need to create their own entry on the database (although they can do this if they feel it is necessary): a user will do this for them through creating a spot and checking-in to that spot.[12] If a spot is created for a restaurant a drinks manufacturer could directly advertise to a user within that restaurant that has checked-in there, or an offer on a meal could be made by the restaurant itself (a feature of the Foursquare application). Moreover, the database collects information on individual users – where they visit, when they visit there, and what they do there depending on the comments that a user contributes to the check-in (which would be invaluable demographic information), but also information that could be used to target the individual in the same way Facebook or Google collects data on usage to sell to advertisers. Barreneche (2012) argues that this classification, built upon an ontology of business-based vocabularies, is vital to an emerging form of economic governance of population mobility flows. This classification enables a particular mode of knowing the world that comes from the embodiment of a particular worldview. In Barreneche's view, this point of interest ontology mirrors a neo-liberal urban politics of privatisation and the disappearance of public space. The database is populated with user-generated content, there is a clear commercial and capitalistic logic to the assemblage of data around business and commercially-oriented mobilities (Evans, 2013).

From top-down to bottom-up

The development of a database of places is indicative of a movement from (i) *representation of location* to (ii) *navigation of places* in mapping. In outlining the development of the OS, mapping was a project that satisfied the political and economic wills of dominant elites within British society. The product of that process, the map, is an inscription of the physical territory but it is an inscription that denotes power relationships, and ascribes them to specific territories within the territory mapped. The function of the representation is not just to locate oneself and to find out where one might want to go, as the map serves as an inscription of power in the world. When one creates a place on Foursquare, there is not a top-down power relationship in the cartography. The creation of a gazetteer or database entry is both down to the users of the network (and therefore distributed rather than concentrated in the hands of a cartographer) and immediately turned over to the network[13] as a bottom-up (i.e. users creating the database rather than being "given" the information) form of activity. The map is not a static representation of the territory: the user can add to the map, and change the character of the gazetteers that have already been left on that map. The method of creation and the role of the user have been changed with the role of the map itself. Maps were representations of territory but with the right computational device, maps are something with which we can navigate the world socially and add to, in order to aid others that aim to navigate that physical space. In doing this, the user is actively involved in a transformation of physical space into social place, through the activity of mapping and navigating – the map is literally ontogenetic.

(Latour et al., 2010: 581), and a movement from Korzybski's notion of the map not representing territory to Siegert's (2011: 13) argument that maps can be considered as a space for representation in itself, and a way of understanding the epistemic orders that compete with other epistemic orders in the prioritisation of places and gazetteers. Traditional maps are a representational form offering a graphical representation of territory, and GPS presents all space as co-ordinate, reducing territory to data to be used and circulated. LBSNs reveal the location of the user in relation to the location of other users of the application, in relation to the previous comments, and impressions of venues from other users and in relation to other places in the database. This kind of revealing challenges Radloff's (2007: 44) critique of new mapping techniques: that the representational dissolves into the planetary.

In a technological way of understanding place, as exemplified by GPS, all location is "flattened" and place is not revealed as all locations are revealed "spatially," in relation to one another. In the revealing that occurs with LBSN, the user can be understood as at the centre of the revealing of place: location can be understood as a letting-come-forth from the position of the user relative to places and things in the world, through the thing that is the computational device and LBSN. There is the possibility that the revealing of location is a *poesis*, that is reflected in the semantic, personal and social nature of the gazetteers created by users denote places that are meaningful and gather aspects of the world rather than stand in featureless spatial relation to other gazetteers. As such, there is the possibility that the form of cartography that layers the social and user-generated upon the overtly technological GPS co-ordinate may allow for a way of understanding of place that is closer to the letting-come-forth than the standing-forth as resource. An understanding of the phenomenological orientation to place, practices of use and relationship with the technology itself is necessary to explain how this is possible. This is the focus of the next two chapters, as a digital post-phenomenology of place is constructed to explain how LBSN can assist users in understanding place as *place*.

3
The Phenomenology of Place

This chapter provides a brief exegesis of understanding of place in Heidegger's philosophy from the equipmental spatiality of *Being and Time*, the danger of modern technology and technicity to understanding place through the role of "the thing" as a gathering entity through its "thinging." The purpose of this is to support the contention that the use of things in the world is critical to the understanding of place in contrast to the "industrial" or modernist notion. This account moves across the philosophical thinking of Heidegger, and in doing so acknowledges the change (more famously "the Turn") in Heidegger's thought regarding place while retaining elements of Heidegger's fundamental ontology in *Being and Time* in an overall account of how people understand place through the usage of things in the world.

This analysis emphasises the importance of *care* and bringing things into care as key to understanding place in Heidegger's philosophy as equipmordial spatiality in *Being and Time*. In this book, care and the bringing of the computational device into care is seen as key to understanding how an appreciation of place is achieved using LBSN. Heidegger's own identification of the problem with the primordial orientation to the world or *Befindlichkeit* as a technological worldview (*Weltbilt*) or technological orientation to the world is considered as an obstruction to the possibility of taking things into care that is crucial for understanding place. This technological orientation to the world affects the possibility of what he calls an *attunement* with things that allows for the poetic revealing of place, and reveals things (and place) as resource. The poetic revealing of place emerges from an event (*Ereingis*) where the key elements of world are gathered and Dasein can understand the world as place through taking things into care – including computational devices.

This brief account of the key concepts in Heidegger's work is therefore intended as a introduction to the key concepts of phenomenology that will guide the analysis of responses from the ethnography of Foursquare users in Chapters 5 and 6. The concepts that are introduced in this chapter are foundational in the post-phenomenological framework that is proposed in this book; a necessary but not sufficient element in that framework, as the basic orientation to things explained as mood in this chapter plays a critical role in the manner of post-phenomenological engagement and understanding that will be explained through Chapter 4.

A brief introduction to Heidegger's thought

Heidegger has been hailed as one of the most important philosophers of the 20th century and as such has been hugely influential on a number of subsequent philosophers, thinkers, cultural theorists and media researchers (e.g. Scannell, 1995; Gunkel and Taylor, 2014). This chapter focuses on Heidegger's notion of space and place, from his work in *Being and Time*, to the so-called later Heidegger. Heidegger's particular position on space is informed though his phenomenological approach, itself largely influenced by his love of and romanticisation of German rural life. Thus his work lies at the crossroads between the rural norms of place and those represented in the industrial and highly capitalist world represented by urban living. Within this approach there is a clear difference between what Heidegger interprets as a mode of being (or being-in-the-world) that allows for the revealing of place and a mode that reveals space, with space corresponding to a modernist, scientific understanding of location and the world of human action. This modernist or technological mode of revealing reveals location as space, as something to be used as resource and without an essential meaning that derives from taking other entities into consideration and thinking about the nature and meaning of that location. The revealing of place, where entities are revealed as entities and not mere resource, is an understanding of location that emerges from allowing other entities to be seen as part of a referential totality of things within that region. This comes from an attunement or being-towards the world that seeks to understand place as *place*, and this attunement is what Heidegger calls (in his later work) *dwelling*.

Heidegger's original project was to understand being; this chapter argues that this understanding is dependent upon proper dwelling in the world, and that dwelling is a relationship to other things that allows for a poetic revealing of the world. Understanding of being is a function of dwelling in the world, but this dwelling needs to be understood in reference not only to things but also to Dasein's taking up of things into care. By taking things into care Dasein stands in relation to that thing and uses the thing in fulfilling a towards-which, and that is part of Dasein's attunement as dwelling. This means that Dasein's engagement with things is part of the clearing (*lichtung*, the clearing away of ontotheology and assessment of being *as* being), but not what the clearing is. The clearing is the ground for Dasein's understanding of place, but Dasein's access to that clearing is through its use of things in a manner that allows for the revealing of place to occur. In the context of computational objects, it is the manner of use in locating oneself in a place that will be part of Dasein's attunement or dwelling in place, and as such there will be practices of use that are conducive towards dwelling and some practices that will be indicative of a technological mode of revealing.

Equipmental understanding of place – The understanding of place in Being and Time

While accepting that Heidegger's fundamental ontology privileges being as temporal, following Malpas (2008: 112–146), one can argue that Dasein's understanding of the world (which it is thrown into and necessarily is being-in) through taking objects into care (*Sorge*) and being involved with the world through engagement with equipment (Concern or *Besorge*) is critical to understanding how Dasein makes sense of place. Dasein's making sense of the world is dependent on the mood of Dasein's being-in-the-world, and this mood of situatedness is an attunement to things in the world. Dasein's situatedness is a "being-there" that resonates with or is attuned to the world through Dasein's own active engagement in the world (Malpas, 2008: 126). The kind of understanding of space is an existential nearness or distance to place, is dependent upon the bringing things into care that is realised as a situateness or attunement to things in the world.

The understanding of place that Dasein achieves through being-with things is critical in understanding not only "being-there" in the context of the "there," but also the manner of being-in that Dasein experiences the world. World in this understanding is not the extended containment of space around the person, but the relational involvement that Dasein has to things in the world, and how Dasein stands in relation to things in the world. World is a meaningful existential locale for Dasein, and the relationship between humans and other entities in the world and Dasein's engagement with other entities affects its understanding of the world and place. While Heidegger's treatment of Dasein in *Being and Time* has been criticised due to the transcendental subjectivity of Dasein as a world-revealing entity,[1] the ideas of equipmentality and the taking up of equipment into care through engagement are key to understanding how humans engage with things to create the conditions for understanding place. This chapter moves from *world* as a meaningful place where Dasein stands in relation to other things, as an entity concerned with its own being, to an exegesis of Heidegger's fundamental ontology with attention to care as the ontological and ontic structure of Dasein, to how care is critical in understanding place. The intention is to lay bare the basics of a phenomenology of place: care, attunement and situatedness.

Heidegger's fundamental ontology and spatiality

The fundamental ontology of Being in Heidegger's *Being and Time* is temporal: Dasein is a temporal entity and time is the transcendental horizon for the question of being (Kockelmans, 1970: 319).[2] Given this, the role of the spatial in Heidegger's fundamental ontology would be expected to be secondary; humans are the only entities for which time is a factor in being-in-the-world. Other entities, such as physical objects are merely present-at-hand objects with no concept of time. Given this temporal primacy, the role of spatiality needs to be understood in the context of this revealing and unveiling. Spatiality is revealed through the existence of Dasein in time and in-the-world as a temporal being.

One might feel that the natural sciences are suitable for understanding place. The unsuitability of empirical or positivist approaches arises from a conflation of the terms universe and world (Wrathall, 2006: 20). The physical sciences deal with the universe successfully, and it is to those disciplines that we should look to explain the physical interactions of bodies in the universe. The universe is not the same thing as the world though; for Heidegger, the world is a genuine phenomenon in its own right and is not something that can be reduced to the physical objects that make up that world. The world is something that has meaning to us and that we understand.[3] The scientific facts of the world emerge from a particular comportment towards the world and a particular circumspection, and are not holistic truths (Dreyfus, 1990: 74). Indeed, Dreyfus points out that the scientific reductionism that Heidegger wants to avoid is a product of Cartesian *res extensa*: it tells us how a hammer works but not what its meaning is, and so provides an impoverished view of the world (Dreyfus, 1990: 112). The world is full of meaning, and as a "being-in-the-world" Dasein understands these meanings.[4] As Dasein, we always comport ourselves towards this place called the world; always striving to understand meaning and act accordingly (Dreyfus, 1990: 99). The world is then a referential whole, and we understand entities through this referential whole and the references between entities, not through the intentional study of individual actors or objects in the world (Dreyfus, 1990:103).[5]

While the universe can be described using the term space (and therefore linked to the material extension of Cartesian dualism) the world for Dasein is a place; somewhere that Dasein resides and lives. Contrast my office and a war zone: both are examples of places for Dasein, one a place of familiarity and the other a place of unfamiliarity. My "appropriateness" for each place marks my ability to effectively be in each place. The objects that make up each place are different, and the actions that are typical in each place are also different, but they are both places. This concept of the world is one that explicitly brings practices into consideration. The world is not just spatial or physical, but is semantically meaningful through the interactions that persons have with others and other objects in that world.

Place is not an objective, spatial, geometric phenomenon like the Cartesian explanation – places are existential locales (Blattner, 2007: 75), or world. Familiarity with such places is a sense of nearness or distance, but existential rather than geometric distance.[6] From Heidegger's phenomenological perspective, we are not located in space-time. Instead, we are always somewhere more or less familiar. Dasein, and disclosure-as-such which provides the identity of Dasein to itself and other entities, is dependent on such existential locales. The idea of existential locales avoids issues with consciousness as phenomena by explaining conscious phenomena as part of the world rather than a disembodied process. We are familiar with objects and places due to our experiences of them, not by holding them in an intentional manner in the mind, or considering them in abstract cognitive ways. There is no need to posit mental explanations for how we consider different entities with greater or lesser depth, as this can be explained by the familiarity that we have with them through experience.[7] The existentially near place is somewhere Dasein understands through its disclosing of the place as place, and the existentially far space is somewhere that Dasein is unfamiliar with due to the character of its involvement with the other entities in that place.[8]

Care and the care structure as equipmental spatiality

Heidegger explains how Dasein is in the world – how it is involved with the world and the entities in that world – through the concept of care.

Care (*Sorge*) is "the structure of Dasein itself" (Heidegger, 1992: 293), and is both an existential (ontic) and ontological category of Dasein, as Dasein necessarily cares for the world through its involvements with equipment (Concern; *Besorge*) and being-with others (*Fürsorgen*). Care is part of the structure of Dasein as a thing in itself (ontologically), and existentially is how Dasein is related to the world through its care for the world: "The authentic relation of the world and Dasein is care and meaningfulness" (Heidegger, 1992: 221).

Care as concern is the relationship between Dasein and entities that are not-Dasein – that is, other things in the world. Care is therefore not only concerned with Dasein and other entities that are Dasein (other humans), but also with equipment and things or objects in the world. Care is a pre-cognitive or *a priori*-ontological relation to the world (Heidegger, 1962: 244) and is not chosen by Dasein but is a constitutive part of Dasein: the existential position of being-with-things is inevitable, as an ontological truth of Dasein. Care is therefore a universal phenomenon of Dasein – unavoidable, unchangeable – that as part of the ontological structure of Dasein shapes the ontic interpretation of the world. The understanding of the world is the question for Dasein. In this sense, care is the means by which Dasein understands the world, and this understanding is through being-in-the-world. Dasein does not understand the world through a rational detachment from space or a calculative detachment, but is ontologically part of the world (situated in the world) and understands the world and being from this position.

Explicitly, care as a constituent of the ontological structure of Dasein and existential relation to the world (ontic) is the spatiality of Dasein. It is through care that Dasein is necessarily in the world (ontologically) and engaged with the other things and entities that it encounters in the world (ontically). The facticity of Dasein's being in the world is care:

> The transcendental "universality" of the phenomenon of care and all fundamental existentials has, on the other hand, that broad scope through which the basis is given on which every ontic interpretation of Dasein with a worldview moves, whether it understands Dasein as "the cares of life" and need, or in an opposite manner. (Heidegger, 1962: 244)

This ontological structure of Dasein as care necessarily situates Dasein in the world. Care also illustrates that Dasein is not a simple substance in the world, but a complex being that through the ontological structure of care is a unified in its articulation as Dasein itself and in the world, avoiding substance dualism:

> The "emptiness" and "generality" of the existential structures which obtrude themselves ontically have their own ontological definiteness and fullness. The whole of the constitution of Dasein itself is not simple in its unity, but shows a structural articulation which is expressed in the existential concept of care. (Heidegger, 1962: 244)

Care acts as the unifying characteristic of Dasein, both in the ontological-ontic difference and the temporal-spatial. While Dasein is a temporal entity, its temporality is one that requires spatial presence in the world with other things and other entities. Care is the answer to the question of the understanding of being, in that the existential analytic of what is it to be in the world is answered through care, and that this answer also leads back to the ontology of Dasein:

> Our ontological interpretation of Dasein has brought the pre-onto-logical self-interpretation of this being as "care" to the existential concept of care. The analytic of Dasein does not aim, however, at an ontological basis for anthropology; it has a fundamental, ontological goal. This is the purpose that has inexplicitly determined the course of our considerations, our choice of phenomena, and the limits to which our analysis may penetrate. (Heidegger, 1962: 238)

Heidegger makes explicit that the understanding of care is not something that should lead to a concentration on analysis at the ontic level (anthropology), but that the understanding of being is something that needs to be understood on the basis of the importance of the care structure of Dasein. The phenomena for understanding being-in-the-world should be those that arise from the analytic of care. The importance of care not only structurally for Dasein, but also for the understanding of being should now be clear.

> The *perfectio* of human being – becoming what one can be in being free for one's own most possibilities (project) – is an "accomplishment" of "care". But, equiprimordially, care determines the fundamental mode of this being according to which it is delivered over (thrownness) to the world taken care of. The "ambiguity" of "care" means a *single* basic constitution in its essentially twofold structure of thrown project. (Heidegger 1962: 243)

The possibility of perfect being – which is becoming free and realising the possibilities of one's own being[9] – is dependent upon Dasein's care for the world and achieving care in an existential sense. Care is identified as essential to the mode of being-in-the-world,[10] as in how is Dasein in the world and how does it engage with other things in the world. The very possibility of understanding the world (and place) is through care.

Dasein's being in the world must be "as" something, or in a particular manner. The manner in which Dasein discloses itself to other entities and understands other entities in the world is critical in understanding how the world as an existential space inhabited by other things and entities is understood. Significantly, the notion that there are ways, plural rather than singular, of being-in is important: an analysis of the potential ways of being-in-the-world and how these moods (*stimmung*) of Dasein affect Dasein's understanding of place is required:

> We must now make an existential-analytical inquiry as to the temporal conditions, for the possibility of the spatiality that is characteristic of Dasein – the spatiality upon which in turn is founded the uncovering of space within-the-world. We must first remember in what way Dasein is spatial. Dasein can be spatial only as care, in the sense of existing as factically falling. Negatively this means that Dasein is never present-at-hand in space, not even proximally. Dasein does not fill up a bit of space as a Real Thing or item of equipment would, so that the boundaries dividing it from the surrounding space would themselves just define that space spatially. Dasein takes space in; this is to be understood literally. It is by no means just present-at-hand in a bit of space which its body fills up. In existing, it has already made room for its own leeway. (Heidegger, 1962: 419)

Heidegger makes it clear that Dasein can be spatial only as care, but that spatiality is not the same as the spatiality of a thing or item of equipment. In Heidegger's fundamental ontology, care is how Dasein *acts* as an entity towards other entities in the world. In other words Dasein's engagement with things is through the ontological structure of Dasein as care.

The "world" is a place that Dasein acts in, in accordance with understanding how actions can be performed and with which equipment those actions can be effectively achieved in this world. For Dasein, there are many worlds and the appropriateness of the world will vary due to the understanding of Dasein and their familiarity with the world within which it is situated. The understanding that Dasein has is not factual – that is the knowledge derived from empirical or positivist observation that is the method of the empirical sciences – but is instead an understanding rooted in the way Dasein does things. An understanding of carpentry is shown in the way I handle a hammer and nails, and construct something from wood, not from my knowledge of the physical properties of the wood.[11] Dasein's understanding of the world does not come from a factual understanding of the world, but instead *knowing how* to live in the world. Familiarity with the world comes with understanding why things are done in the manner in which they are done in the world.

The moods of being-in-the-world: Situatedness and attunement

This account of world may be seen as problematic, in that it does not immediately offer an explanation of how Dasein's engagement with things can be meaningful, or how it is not always meaningful; change over time is not explained.[12] In order to understand why understanding the world occurs or does not occur, the manner of Dasein's engagement with things in the world as well as the functional use of things requires examination. Dasein's mood of engagement with the world or attunement to the world is the primordial condition of "being-attuned" as a basic condition of being (Coyne, 2010: xiv) and this mood of being-in-the-world explains how and why Dasein makes sense of place by bringing things into care, creating particular existential locales. For Heidegger, mood (*Stimmung*) is our attunement towards the world. Dasein is already in the world and as such cannot have a neutral attunement towards it.

> It [Dasein] finds itself in this way or that way it is disposed in this or that mood. When we say it finds itself, this "itself" first does not really refer expressly to a developed and thematically conscious I. (Heidegger, 1992: 255)

Heidegger uses the concept of attunement (*Befindlichkeit*)[13] as it relates to mood to explain this. Mood is not something chosen, as Dasein does not choose to be bored or anxious; it is bored or anxious. Jacobson (2006: 94) argues that the spatial understanding of Dasein changes with mood, as mood discloses the way that Dasein exists as being-in. When an "objectively" identical thing or region is significant in one instance and insignificant in another, then it is the mood or orientation to the world of Dasein that is responsible for this change.[14]

Dasein is always in a mood of some kind, and is always therefore oriented to the world in some way. When understood as an *attunement* to things, Dasein's mood or towards-which in the world will direct Dasein's circumspection towards things in the world. The taking of things into care as ready-to-hand is due to the towards-which that Dasein is in at that time. It is this kind of engagement or attunement that I argue is responsible for a revealing of place. If Dasein is in a mood where its "mineness" is *lost*[15], Dasein's care is *lost* and falls into the world of the "They" (Inwood, 2002: 23–24). In such a towards-which, Dasein does not see its "mineness" in the context of its possibilities (those possibilities that are ahead of itself as a towards-which), but instead defines itself in the terms of the "They" (Inwood, 2002: 23). This kind of engagement or mood is what Heidegger saw as the result of a technological mode of existence, a being-towards the world that sets the world (and those entities within it) as resources to be used.

The question concerning technology and the annihilation of thinking about place

As care is critical to thinking about place, the means by which Heidegger believes care is "lost" in the modern epoch, and how this affects the revealing of place is important. Equipmental spatiality is threatened by what Heidegger identifies as the essence of modern technology, enframing. Enframing is an orientation to the world and other entities that frames other entities as resources to be used. This enframing gives Being the perspective that other entities do not have a deeper, fixed essence of their own, but are simply a resource, framed as "standing reserve", to be utilised maximally when necessary. In the context of this work, space itself would have no further meaning than being a resource, and the kind of meaningful place (world or existential space) that Heidegger argued is the place of Dasein's proper dwelling would not be understood in a technological world-revealing. With all space revealed as resource, the kind of meaningful understanding from the engagement with things through care would not occur in this world orientation.

Enframing is for Heidegger a great danger for being; such an orientation to the world does not allow humans to correctly interpret how the natural world and other entities disclose themselves to humans, and as such is an important phenomenological concept. This section aims to show how this technological world-revealing obscures the kind of world-revealing that comes from the use of things when taken into care.

The essence of technology, for Heidegger, is something that prevents us from having a proper understanding of our own being. Heidegger's philosophy after "the turn" is the history of being (Gorner, 2006), or *seingeschichte*, and the study of technology is a study in the history of being. The fundamental difference after the "turn" is in how being is considered, not as something in itself but as something that affects the ability of being to understand itself.[16] Heidegger's aim in "The Question Concerning Technology" is set out in the first paragraph (Heidegger, 1977: 3): to investigate technology in order to prepare us for a "free relationship" with technology. Heidegger's major concern is how "we" relate to technology, how we think about it and how it affects us. Heidegger is not concerned with the existence of technology, but instead how humans are orientated towards technology. The problem is not the technology itself, and so the problem cannot be resolved through improving technology:

> Thus we shall never experience our relationship to the essence of technology so long as we merely conceive and push forward the technological, put up with it, or evade it. Everywhere we remain unfree and chained to technology, whether we passionately affirm or deny it. (Heidegger, 1977: 3)

Heidegger accepts that technology cannot be avoided or escaped, and so must be considered. More importantly, Heidegger asserts that the essence of technology is not "anything technological" either (Heidegger, 1977: 4). This assertion serves the purpose of opening up technology for discussion free from the domain of technological experts, and towards the field of philosophy. The removal of technology from the essence of technology also allows Heidegger to undertake a historical analysis of technology, including an analysis of Greek philosophy, and to argue that the essence of technology precedes the emergence of modern technology in the 18th century.

Heidegger's analysis of technology

The analysis of technology begins by questioning how humans think about technology. Heidegger divides definitions of technology into *instrumental* and *anthropological* definitions of technology (Heidegger, 1977: 5). Such definitions do not go far enough for Heidegger; in effect, the definitions of technology based on the pragmatics of technology create a "blind spot" that prevents further understanding.[17] Thinking about technology is dominated by what the technology does and how humans use the technology, rather than by how the technology affects being and what the relationship is between humans and technology.

To understand how being and humans stand in relationship to technology, Heidegger considers what is meant by the "instrumental" use of technology as a means to an end. From causation, and the *aition* being that which is responsible for something else, Heidegger (1977: 11) introduces the term *poesis*, which is related to being responsible for something in the sense that the silversmith is responsible for the chalice. *Poesis* means "bringing forth," and Heidegger means two things by bringing forth; the first being the bringing forth into existence, such as a silversmith practices with a chalice, and the second being the bringing forth into nature, such as a tree that is brought forth from the acorn. Both kinds are *poesis*, in the way in which something was brought forth which was not present. "Bringing-forth brings out of concealment into unconcealment" (Heidegger 1977: 11). The understanding of *poesis* as a kind of revealing led Heidegger to conclude that it is related to the Greek word *aletheia*, which means "revealing" and is also the Greek word for truth. Clearly Heidegger argues that technology is a kind of *poesis*, a way of bringing forth from concealment, and as such is in "the realm of truth" (Heidegger, 1977: 12). The word *poesis* alludes to poetry and it is not as incongruent as Heidegger is looking for an alternative method to thinking about technology, away from instrumentality, and the way that *poetry* confronts the world and relates to human beings is radically different from the way that instrumentality frames and confronts the world.

Technology comes from the Greek *technikon*, which is related to the word *techne*. Heidegger argues that *techne* refers to both manufacturing and the arts, such as the techniques of artists and poets. *Techne* also relates to *episteme*, from which epistemology derives, as to how we know things. *Techne* is therefore a kind of knowing of things and the world; the "know-how" or the revealing of knowing how things are done (Heidegger, 1977). If technology is understood as deriving from this sense of *techne* then the essence of technology can be seen not in the instrumental production of things or the instrumental use of things but as a revealing of how things are known. The silversmith, through his *techne*, brings together the form and the matter of the chalice, and the idea of the chalice to reveal the chalice that has been on its way to existence.[18]

Technology has traditionally been a *poesis* that brings forth what has not been present, such as the windmill that harnesses the power of the wind. The wind is there, but the power of the wind requires the technology to be revealed forth. Modern technology does not act in the way of bringing forth, but instead extracts and exploits, such as the changing of the earth by mining coal into a resource, which cannot be repaired or restored to its former state. Heidegger also uses the example of the Rhine River to draw the comparison between modern technology and the "revealing" of poetry. When the river is dammed to provide electricity, the meaning of the river is altered; it becomes a resource for energy. The view of the Rhine as a source of hydroelectric power is contrasted with the poetry of Höderlin, whose poetry portrays the river as a source of artistic, philosophical and nationalistic inspiration. The source of revealing is the same in both cases, but the result of the revealing is clearly different. Modern technology reveals, but the revealing is of a different kind to the *poesis*. To explain this further, Heidegger introduces the notion of the standing reserve.

Standing reserve and enframing

Enframing describes how humans come to relate to the world around them, or how they are orientated to the world around them. Heidegger explains *Gestell* as a type of schematic structure; something that organises our perceptions in a manner that informs our understanding of the world. Thus, enframing compels humans to categorise our experiences and the entities that we encounter in the world. This then gives humans a sense of control over the entities that are encountered in the world, and it is this that is the character of modern technology. To refer to the history of being, this kind of understanding of the world is one where all things are organised as resource, and all things are revealed as things to be used and no more than that.

Heidegger states that the essence of modern technology "is by no means anything technological" (Heidegger, 1977: 4). Technology does not have its essence in technological creations themselves, and not in the activities that humans indulge in using technology, such as creating LBSNs. Instead, the essence of technology is realised through the "frame of mind" or attunement (*Befindlichkeit*) in which the individual constituents of technological processes are viewed. Here, therefore, I would argue in relation to computational devices, that neither the device nor the user are the "essence" of the technology, as such, but they can be understood as the *standing reserve* or the parts of this relationship as an interaction – hence the technology and the users are viewed as raw materials for another product. People using smartphones and geolocational applications can be ordered by the technology into a relationship not only with the other users but also with the technology itself.

Enframing is a process of reduction in that humans are reduced to resources, and the inherent significance of entities will be lost due to this reductive process (Wrathall, 2007: 82). As Heidegger notes, humans go from being entities with deep essences to "functionaries of enframing" (Heidegger, 1947: 30). As functionaries of enframing, humans are affected in two ways. Firstly, they are transformed into resources to be exploited by other users. Secondly humans will be driven to get the most out of the possibilities that exist in other people. In doing this, the deep essences of other entities will not be recognised and other entities are simply seen in terms of their ease of use and maximum utility, and how flexible the entity is in being used for the needs of the person. Such a revealing "never comes to an end" (Heidegger, 1977: 16) because everything must be considered as a resource at all times.

Modern technology, by having the essence of enframing and reducing entities to standing reserve, changes the sense that humans have for the world (Wrathall, 2007: 101). Heidegger uses the example of farming to illustrate this (Wrathall, 2007: 102). Farming was a vocation, the purpose of which was to tend and care for the land that the farming took place on. When farming became a mechanised industry, with no notion of stewardship,[19] the ability of a farmer to look after nature was reduced. Indeed, the enframing of modern technology sets out something other than maintenance. It is also the role of the farmer to improve nature, not maintain it. If nature is improved by modern technology, then humans are no longer constrained by nature as they can change it, do with it what they want and extract whatever is needed from it due to its status as a resource. An understanding of physical space that can be utilised for maximum reward supersedes an understanding of place,[20] and this clearly relates to the pertinent issue of the understanding of place in this thesis. This is very different to the revealing of place through the taking of things into care proposed in Chapter 5, and as such represents a danger as place is ostensibly eradicated from understanding of the world, through the obscuring of care for things (concern) by the totalising worldview that is the technological mode of revealing.

Things, thinging and dwelling – Spatiality in the later Heidegger

There is an understanding of spatiality in Heidegger's later philosophy that both consolidates and addresses problems in the phenomenological understanding of spatiality derived from *Being and Time* while also addressing the affect of the technological worldview. The technological world-revealing is an annihilation of the taking into care that is critical to a poetic revealing of place[21] or revealing of location as letting-come forth or *poesis*. The problematic aspect of Heidegger's fundamental ontology is that it conceived of Dasein as an ahistorical entity that gives meaning to the world through its presence as a worlding or world-revealing entity. This view gives no role to the things, or orientation to things that Dasein has, or arrangement of things in the world that have a role in making a space meaningful as a place. Malpas (2008: 156) summarises the problem: "the account set out in *Being and Time* seems to make spatiality, for instance, dependent on the projective activity, ultimately grounded in temporality, of individual being-there. It also indicates the way in which the emphasis on meaning and projective understanding threatens to make problematic the relation between being-there and world."

In doing this, dwelling is understood as part of an event that reveals world as place. In the next chapter I will provide an exegesis of the key ideas pertaining to spatiality in Heidegger's later work concerning The Thing (*Das Ting*), The Event (*Ereignis*) and the Fourfold (*Das Geviert*). These three concepts are constituent in understanding the concept of dwelling as a way of being-in-the-world, and position dwelling as the attunement to the world or Dasein's mood that is conducive to establishing a sense of place in the world. The idea that man (or Dasein) dwells in the world, and that this dwelling is conducive to a proper understanding of things (and hence a proper understanding of being) is critical to the phenomenological position established in this chapter.

The mood or attunement of Dasein to the world that is dwelling is not a projection of Dasein onto the world, but is emergent through Dasein's engagement with the world and the structure of things in that world. These elements are gathered together in an event, and dwelling is a factor of both Dasein's towards-which and the things Dasein encounters and uses in the world. Taking things into care makes possible the attunement of dwelling as a means of making sense of location that allows Dasein to be claimed by that place and to think about location in a manner that is not as resource but that takes other entities into consideration as entities rather than objects.

The problem of transcendence

The account of understanding place from *Being and Time* is dependent upon Dasein as a world-revealing entity through its engagement with things. The involvement or engagement with things is critical to how Dasein makes sense of place in a world of computational things, but that the concept of care cannot be ignored. As a transcendental, world-revealing being there is no necessity for Dasein to deal with things at all, but this suggests all world-revealing is dependent upon Dasein (and therefore is arbitrary or mysterious) or that the technological changes throughout time have had no effect on world-revealing which of course makes no sense given Heidegger's own position on the history of being. Heidegger's philosophy after "the turn" is the history of being (Gorner, 2006), or *Seingeschichte*; the turn (*Kehre*) is the addressing of the question of being as how Dasein or being-there and being stand in relation to one another. In effect this is a reorientation of Heidegger's thought that Heidegger himself saw as necessary[22]:

> I attempted in *Being and Time* to provide a preliminary characteriza-
> tion of the *phenomenon of world* by interpreting *the way in which we
> at first and for the most part move about in our everyday world.* There
> I took my departure from what lies to hand in the everyday realm,
> from those things that we use and pursue ... In and through this
> initial characterization of the phenomenon of world the task is to
> press on and to point out the phenomenon of world as a problem. It
> never occurred to me, however, to try and claim or prove with this
> interpretation that the essence of man consists in the fact that he
> knows how to handle knives and forks or use the tram. (Heidegger,
> 1995: 177; in Dreyfus and Wrathall, 2009: 365)

Two things must be taken from this view. Firstly, the idea of taking things into care is still a part of the understanding of the phenomenon of world, but it is only the primary movement of Dasein to world. As such, it is indispensible to an understanding of world, but is not in itself an understanding of world. Secondly, there is something beyond the engagement with things that Dasein has when it brings them into care as ready-to-hand tools. The withdrawal of the thing from the conspicu-ousness of Dasein in its use as a tool would seem to limit the role of the tool in how the world is encountered, but the tool does not withdraw totally. Heidegger's notion of the thing "thinging," that is playing a role in gathering elements together (including Dasein's use of the tool in care and the mood of Dasein) is how the thing is brought back to the worlding of Dasein. The thing is central to Dasein's understanding of place through its "thinging," and it is the particular practices of using things that allow for this bringing forth of place, rather than place being revealed as a standing forth.

The concern with the things themselves retains the notions of Dasein as being-there and being-in-the-world while refocusing on the things that Dasein encounters in a world that is populated with computational entities. This return must be made sense of with reference to the tech-nological mode of revealing, with the focus on how Dasein's engage-ment with computational things in trying to understand place avoids or resists this totalising ontotheology. The arrangement of things in the world and the kind of thing Dasein engages with are vital in the under-standing of place that Dasein achieves if it is attuned to the world in a manner that allows such an understanding (that of place, meaningful, rather than space or resource) of place to be achieved.

It is this kind of understanding that marks the turn in Heidegger's thinking after his "turn." The understanding of being is still the key consideration, but the understanding of being as fundamental ontology is one that leads only to a partial or misunderstood conception of being.[23] The clearing (*lichtung*) is where Dasein can reclaim the possibility of thinking about being by being able to think. In a mode of technological revealing Dasein cannot think as all things are revealed as resource, including other entities and Dasein itself, and as such thinking about being is absent in such a world-revealing. The clearing is not a projection of Dasein, but a gathering of Dasein, the place and the things in that place into an event (*Ereignis*). In this way, *Ereignis* is a clearing away of the technological mode of revealing as a totalising world disclosure, and a place for thinking about the deeper essences of things and other entities. In the later Heidegger the taking of things into care as important in understanding place and placehood is not rejected, but seen as only a part of how Dasein is gathered into an understanding of place that avoids the technological world-revealing.

The Thing, event and fourfold

In using *Ereignis*, Heidegger means an event that makes visible the relations between things in the world (including Dasein) as a referential totality.[24] The event here is not just the happening of my being in the world or being-there but the unitary gathering of the basic elements that are constitutive of the world itself (Malpas, 2008: 220).

The gathering of Dasein with other things creates a locale for this revealing or a local place in which Dasein is gathered with other things that are revealed to Dasein within the bounded region of that place and are both part of the meaning of that place and refer to the meaning of that place.[25] This hermeneutic circle of meaning is critical for how I want to understand the event in this work, as the use of things by Dasein in the revealing of location is both a part of that location as revealed as place and part of that place as the region that Dasein is situated in at that time.

Therefore, in the practices that users have in understanding place using LBSN, *there is an event (in the sense of Ereignis) where the key elements of world are gathered and Dasein can understand the world as place through the revealing that comes from bringing forth the location-based social network and the computational device through taking it into care.* The event is a gathering that occurs when a thing "things." For a thing to "thing" it is held "near" to Dasein to create the locale of revealing. This nearness is the circumspection of Dasein as part of taking the thing into care, and therefore the nearness itself (and the event of revealing) is contingent upon taking things into care. The technological world-revealing holds all things as equally distant and close, flattening all things in terms of nearness. This "uniform distancelessness" (Heidegger, 2007: 268) destroys the possibility of a world-revealing event. In the context of the use of LBSN, practices must be considered for how they bring the technology "near" and can be part of a gathering that brings Dasein into a world-revealing moment.

Dwelling represents the possibility of avoiding the modern condition of anxiety and homelessness in the world, and that modern man fails to dwell. By not dwelling, we avoid existential questions about self and identity as we are given easy options to be distracted through the technological mode of revealing (McHugh, 2007: 263).[26] The type of thinking that is desirable for Heidegger is the poetic kind, in that we need to step back from thinking that represents and instead need to think in a manner that recalls and responds to entities themselves (McHugh, 2007: 264). This thinking is difficult because of the mode of technological revealing as there is no requirement to think intuitively or to bring mystery to presence when technology reveals so conveniently. The technological objectification of things in the world leads to a mode of thinking that is incompatible with dwelling, and therefore dwelling itself is a thinking about (or more appropriately an attunement to) entities in the world that allows things to come forth as a letting-come-forth rather than a bringing-forth.

Dwelling is the world as experienced through the fourfold of earth, sky, mortals and divinities (Heidegger, 2008: 247), and this will be explained explicitly with reference to the computational device, LBSN and the Thing in Chapter 4 when Heidegger's phenomenology of place is integrated with a post-phenomenological analysis of the digital world.

Heidegger's position in summary

In *Being and Time*, Dasein is a world-disclosing entity. Without Dasein to act in disclosing the world, then the world does not exist as a referential totality of things that Dasein understands, acting in accordance with that understanding. Dasein does not choose this role: Dasein is necessarily in the world, and this necessity is due to the ontological structure of Dasein as care, that necessarily engages it with the world. In this involvement, Dasein encounters other things as equipment, either as present-at-hand or ready-to-hand tools. When ready-to-hand, the object withdraws from circumspection, but is part of the world-revealing that Dasein does, as the entity for which understanding of the world is a concern. Essentially, Dasein is the entity that brings phenomenal spatial understanding to the world, and it is with reference to Dasein that the world is understood, and by Dasein that the world is understood spatially. Dasein's mood as attunement to the world is essential in the way that Dasein discloses the world to itself, and this attunement or towards-which is how Dasein is oriented to things in order to use them as ready-to-hand tools. The temporal nature of Dasein means that Dasein is always oriented to the world in a particular manner, and this mood situates Dasein in the world – its world-revealing is a function of the mood of Dasein.

A technological understanding of world, that is the comportment or orientation towards the world that views all entities in the world as a resource to be used, prevents this understanding of entities as tools and therefore actively prohibits an understanding of place based on a referential totality of things in a space that can be understood as world in this philosophical view.

The taking up of things into care is critical in understanding how computational devices can reveal place to users, but care alone preserves Dasein as a world-projecting entity. If care is considered as part of the world-revealing event that occurs when a thing "things," then the world-projecting (and open to accusations of solipsism) Dasein can be reconceptualised as an entity that engages with the world and experiences worlding and place through a particular orientation and manner of engagement with things in the world. "Thinging" should be understood as the arranging of elements in the world into a particular orientation that allows for a poetic revealing of place. The taking of the thing into care, along with the comportment to the world of the person, is part of this world-revealing event that is a thinking about place rather than a technological revealing of space. The experience of place (or worldhood) is therefore a function of care and mood as well as the thing and the space being gathered by the thing during a world-revealing attunement (dwelling). As stated earlier, care is the existential (ontic) and ontological structure of Dasein. The next chapter makes explicit how the taking into care (in the ontic or existential sense) of the computational device gives the device the status of a thing that can reveal in this manner. The body and the presence of code and data in the world are necessary conditions for this feeling of place in the digital world. In essence, a post-phenomenology built on this Heideggerian foundation.

4
The Mobile Device as a Thing: The Gathering of Place Digitally

This chapter focuses on the *thing*, in this context the "computational device," and how it is capable of revealing place as place in the digitally mediated world. LBSN can be a "thing" (*Das Ting*) in the sense that Heidegger employs the word, as a world-revealing entity that gathers the necessary elements together to understand world (and place) in an event, and therefore following the theoretical position established in Chapter 3 allows for a dwelling-with technology. Heidegger's Thing is not considered sufficient to explain the feeling of *place*, however, in the context of two important aspects of the digital world: firstly, the interaction and practices of interacting with the computational device and code, and secondly in explaining the presence of data and information in the digital world. As such, this chapter develops a *post-phenomenological* theory with Heidegger's notions of care, mood and situated attunement at the base, but integrating a sense of the body in place and the digital atmosphere. This goes beyond *Dasein* (and hence avoids the possibility of a world-projecting being) by contextualising being-in-the-world as embodied in action in an information-infused environment while retaining being-there as key to understanding the different senses of place that users of LBSN may have through using the technology (and therefore avoiding technological determinism). The chapter will present an exegesis on Heidegger's rather oddly constructed and somewhat mystical-sounding concept of the fourfold (the elements that the "thing" gathers), along with explaining the material and computational functioning of the device that is a "thing." The materiality of the device is then integrated with a view of the body and the hermeneutic, embodied relationship with the device that users have in usage, and a conceptualisation of a code-and data-infused environment that affords the possibility of placehood through using computational devices and LBSN in particular.

Importantly, the construction and functioning of computational code within the device is a condition of the possibility of the device facilitating an appreciation of place, along with the orientation (or towards-which) of the user (see Berry, 2011). The device creates an *existential locale*, but that locale is itself situated in an environment infused with data, information and continuous connectivity to these resources. The framework draws on Sloterdijk's theory of spheres to explain the presence of data and information as an influence on the user. The *digital post-phenomenology of place* that is proposed therefore moves from being-there as a mood, to embodied interaction with the device and an environment of data and information. Code is positioned as the feature of applications and devices that allows access to these digital resources and "world" that enables the possibility of *feeling place*. The aim of this chapter is to clarify and materialise this conceptual structure and develop it within the context of location-based social networking in the following two chapters.

The Thing and Fourfold

Initially, it is necessary to understand what is meant by a "thing" in this account. When a thing "things," it draws together elements in the world in a manner Heidegger called the fourfold (Heidegger, 2008: 243). The idea of the fourfold – earth, sky, mortals, divinities – is a simple oneness (Wrathall, 2006: 112), which is how entities in the world exist if that entity has presence in the world as a thing rather than an object. There is some disagreement amongst commentators on how to interpret the fourfold as a concept.[1] Harman (2002: 190–205) insists on interpreting the fourfold in an extension of his interpretation of all being as akin to the as structure of tools, that is in a constant cycle of withdrawal and revealing. Others, in particular Young (2006) and Wrathall (2006) instead consider the fourfold as the pivotal aspect of Heidegger's concept of dwelling. This account concurs with the latter: if dwelling is the attunement to the world that allows for a poetic revealing of place when one is locating oneself in the world, then attunement is when Dasein understands place as meaningful. This is dependent upon the orientation of things in that place and Dasein's towards-which in that place (the underlying motivation or desire of the user to find out about the place). Essentially, the following questions whether the use of LBSN is a way of attuning to the local world that is a gathering of place.

Things in the world "thing"; they perform the function of "thinging" appropriate to what that thing is and its position in the world. This "thinging" is a part of an event in the world, and its "thinging" and is a gathering of the elements of earth, sky, mortals and divinities known as *das Geviert* or the fourfold (Harman, 2007: 131). For Harman (2007), the thing (when "thinging") produces a nearness to that thing. This nearness is when the thing produces a specific locale for being based around how that thing operates in the world, that is what its function is, how it gathers the elements and how this is given back to being as a revealing of the thing and its region, therefore providing an explanation of the (local) world.

The idea of nearness is vital to the understanding of the gathering (or event) itself and how this gathering related to dwelling. Malpas (2000: 218) argues that distance is the factor by which objects in a region are near or far (dis-stance). It is this dis-stance, the nearness or farness of an object, which decides whether an entity is a thing firstly, and secondly whether that thing can perform its "thinging," with a thing being existentially near in the region or locale. So, a thing is the critical aspect of the region itself in that without a thing, there is no region or locale (and hence the homelessness of man in the technological age). We dwell by attuning ourselves to the local world, and this attunement must be an attuning to things in that locale. This leaves open the possibility that different things "thing" in different ways as different things will be revealed and withdrawn in different ways according to their ontic properties. We dwell with things by not exploiting them, by not mastering them and by not subjugating them under our control (as we would if treating things as resource in a technological mode of understanding).

If this is the case, then the way of being-with things can be considered an extension of the existential structure of being-in-the-world as care (Heidegger, 1992: 293) from *Being and Time*. Care is the temporal structure of being-in-the-world – in care we are concerned with the heritage of a thing (past), the involvement with equipment and Dasein (present) and the future. This temporal structure is in evidence with care for the thing in dwelling as we are aware of the thing as a thing (past), involved with the thing (present) and allow in its unfolding and revealing a role for the thing in the future. The fundamental character of dwelling is caring for and protecting things (Young, 2000: 189) and hence being-with things is to take things into being and hold them as concern. The character of the "thinging" is a function of the gathering of the elements of the fourfold. The following illustration is the fourfold:

This structure is a starting point for understanding these elements and eventually how the thing "things" (Figure 4.1). The four elements are earth, sky, gods and mortals,[2] as their relationship is along two axes of

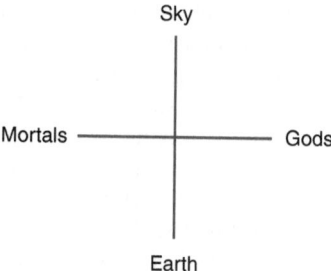

Figure 4.1 Heidegger's fourfold

earth-sky and mortals-divinities. The intersection of the four elements is the event or *Ereignis*. The analysis of the fourfold here concurs with Dreyfus and Spinoza (1997) who argue that when things "thing" they are bringing together these four elements. A local world occurs when an everyday thing "things" and temporarily brings things and people into their own appropriation.

In this view, the elements are significantly simpler than in other accounts (cf. Young 2002; Harman 2007). The taken-for-granted practices that ground situations and give them significance as situations are *earth*. These practices, such as in Borgmann's (in Dreyfus and Spinoza, 1997) example of the family meal, operate to make the gathering significant in that for a family such a dining practice is not an option to indulge in or not, but the basis upon which other options appear (Dreyfus and Spinoza, 1997) and in this thesis as the practices for locating oneself, such as the check-in to Foursquare or the use of the Google map to orient oneself. Heidegger regards this grounding of practices as withdrawn and hidden, whereas *sky* is the revealed or manifest possibilities that arise from the focal situations (such as the family meal) and therefore is explicitly revealed. These are the possibilities for action that are appropriate for that focal gathering or locale in the case of the family meal, discussion of the day and warm conversation would be appropriate (Dreyfus and Spinoza, 1997) while discussion of gory injury and death threats would not be appropriate. The possibilities of action are dictated by the situation which itself is disclosed by the fourfold.

By *divinities* Heidegger refers to the attunement of being in the situation to an extent that one feels in tune with what is happening and events unfold of their own accord without the need to push this unfolding through action. When a thing "things," this sense of divinity must be present, although this too will be withdrawn (Harman, 2007: 132), such as the attunement of dwelling, which should not be thought of as explicit but as the mood in which Dasein is in at that time, pre-reflectively. *Mortals* refers to how the thing "thinging" includes humans but in a specific sense. Obviously, the mortals will be revealed, but also act as disclosers of the thing "thinging" – and therefore the fourfold – itself, as without humans there would be no meaning to the gathering of the elements.[3] Moreover, the choice of the word mortal is not accidental; the human revealing the thing and fourfold must be mortal in that they are being-towards-death, and therefore accepting of the finitude of Being, as only in this mode of Being can the disclosive way of being be revealed to us (Dreyfus and Spinoza, 1997). Heidegger also means by mortals an attribute of the way human practices work that causes mortals to understand they have no fixed identity. This understanding is necessary if one is to attune to the locale and nature of practices demanded by the thing "thinging" and the possibilities that are appropriate for that locale (Dreyfus and Spinoza, 1997).

The fourfold is the event of the thing "thinging" as it gathers the four elements, and in doing so reveals a local world of meaning that is dependent upon the thing. Wrathall (2006: 113) summarises Heidegger in that we dwell in the fourfold by "saving the earth, in receiving the sky, in awaiting the divinities and in accompanying the mortals."[4] In doing this, our being-in-the-world is a dwelling rather than a "homeless" or lost state. This fourfold way of living – saving, receiving, awaiting and escorting – cannot happen without things, and being-with things in a way that allows the fourfold both to be revealed and to be accepted into everyday being. This idea of dwelling being a skill is important as it implies that dwelling is something that is learned and therefore not learned in the technological age. In order to dwell in the technological epoch we would need to relearn the skills that are essential to realise dwelling and therefore reclaiming the essence of man, these skills being the practices that are attuned to the fourfold, no longer treating things as objects and consequently as resource.

> The gift of the outpouring is a gift because it stays earth and sky, divinities and mortals. Yet staying is now no longer the mere persisting of something that is here. Staying appropriates. It brings the four into the light of their mutual belonging. From out of staying's simple onefoldness they are betrothed, entrusted to one another. At one in thus being entrusted to one another, they are unconcealed. The gift of the outpouring stays the onefold of the fourfold of the four. And in the poured gift the jug presences as jug. The gift gathers

what belongs to giving: the twofold containing, the container, the void, and the outpouring as donation. What is gathered in the gift gathers itself in appropriately staying the fourfold. This manifold-simple gathering is the jug's presencing. Our language denotes what a gathering is by an ancient word. That word is: thing. The jug's presencing is the pure, giving gathering of the onefold fourfold into a single time-space, a single stay. The jug presences as a thing. The jug is the jug as a thing. But how does the thing presence? The thing things. Thinging gathers. Appropriating the fourfold, it gathers the fourfold's stay, its while, into something that stays for a while: into this thing, that thing. (Heidegger, 1971: 174)

Heidegger holds that different things "thing" with different modes of revealing (Dreyfus and Spinoza, 1997), and so each thing will gather the elements, or gather to itself, in its own way and manner. Dreyfus and Spinoza (1997) outline the possibility of dwelling with technology and a free relationship with technology. If there are local worlds produced by things thinging, then there is logically a multitude of these worlds that could be manifest to humans as things thing in different ways (as they gather in their own way) and that the human passes between these different world as he attunes to different things at different times. This is an opening for considering the possibility of the technological thing thinging; if one can be with a technological device that gathers the fourfold in a way then a local world would emerge from its thinging. This world would have a character that may be defined as technological, but that still could be a local world. Dreyfus and Spinoza (1997) draw attention to Heidegger's analysis of bridges, and in particular to the *autobahn* bridge. While this is the modern, technological bridge it still exhibits a kind of gathering, not only a way of linking as many routes as possible (as resource). The sky is manifest as multiple possibilities (going this way or that); the earth is the possibility of these manifest possible routes, and the practices of crossing and encountering the bridge (albeit this is weak compared to the non-technical thing). The divinities would be the being in tune with technological flexibility, and the mortals would of course be the people using the bridge, aware of its revealing and with the skills appropriate to the world emergent from the "thinging" of the bridge.

Dwelling can be seen as Heidegger's final response to the threat of enframing and holding all entities in standing reserve (Wrathall, 2006: 109). The technological understanding of the world that is enframing reduces all being (the being of entities and the understanding of being) down to resource. In such an understanding we can use what we want with regards to the entities that we encounter in the world, but conversely there is no reason to do anything as all things are just surface; resources to be used and consumed but not to be used in any way to further understanding of the world or in the world. In dwelling, Dasein considers the entities in a locale as meaningful (not just resource) and hence that environment becomes a meaningful *place*.

Beyond the Fourfold: The materiality of the thing

From this account of the thing, LBSN as an application on a mobile computational device should reasonably be considered a thing that is capable of a gathering of the elements of the world into a world-revealing. What the Heideggerian account of the thing does not consider is how the user *interacts* with the thing in their average everydayness, and how these interactions act to attune us to the digital world. The device is used in an embodied manner: fingers, eyes, hands. These are the ways that the device (and therefore the functioning by the execution of code) is accessed. Furthermore, the thing itself interacts with other things (Wi-Fi routers, mobile data masts, databases, processors, GPS satellites, etc.) in its functioning, and most of this occurs beyond the circumspection of the user. Humans use LBSN for a purpose, and that use is materialised in practices of use and situated in places. Two key considerations therefore move this analysis beyond the Heideggerian and towards a *digital post-phenomenology of place*: embodiment, in that practices of use of devices are embodied by humans as we are embodied entities, and attunement to the digital world as an environment of information and data on call. The rest of this chapter discusses these factors before synthesising with the Heideggerian aspects of phenomenology to provide the analytic framework for the ethnography of LBSN users.

The mobile phone has become an essential object for most people in the West (and increasingly globally): it forms a part of everyday practices and routines, and as such it can be considered a "thing."[5] Goggin (2009: 233) emphasises the importance of the haptic, or tactile, design of new mobile phones as a technology as part of this evocative aspect, particularly with the popularity of text messaging which underscores the emphasis on the mobile phone as a "handy" or haptic technology. This haptic design predates the advent of touchscreen interfaces, but it can be argued that the use of the touchscreen to navigate the interface of the smartphone reemphasised and fetishised the haptic nature of the technology in comparison to the use of symbolic keys with multifunctional purposes in pre-touchscreen mobile phones. As such, Goggin

(2009: 233) argues that the iPhone – as an example of the smartphone, which is used for parsimony and as most Foursquare check-ins are performed using smartphones – is a haptic adaption of the mobile phone. While mobile phones have been dependent upon haptic interfaces as a technology since inception (as the precedent telephone has and continues to be) the smartphone with touchscreen re-emphasises and re-prioritises the haptic interface through the increased screen presence and the possibility of gestures to interact with the smartphone interface beyond the pressing of keys in a uniform manner.

In the previous chapter, the notions of ready-to-hand and present-to-hand objects were raised. In the performance of a task, a tool withdraws from circumspection as it is ready-to-hand. In a way, the tool is an extension of the hand in use, no longer held by but part of the action that the hand, body and tool are performing together and which is the focus of the actor. The focus on the hand is important both in its use in the concept of ready-to-hand but also in how smartphones are used: by the hand. Moores (2014: 196) argues that the habituation of usage of the hand with digital technology is an embodied being-at-home or dwelling with the technology with the body oriented to the technology in a particular way. This intimate contact with the technology led Turkle (2007: 9) to describe such technologies as "intimate machines" that are experienced as part of both the self and the external world. The Heideggerian tool analysis, with the withdrawal of the device as it is ready-to-hand in use, is commensurate with this view.

Recent research has justifiably looked at the role of the hand in accessing, using and understanding these technologies in their use. Insights go back much further than the recent, however: Merleau-Ponty argues that habitual practices of use involve the formation of stable dispositional tendencies (Merleau-Ponty, 2002: 168). Ingold (2000: 153) argues that as people necessarily embodied in the world we come to feel our way through a world that is continually coming into being as a consequence of that feeling through. This is not the awareness of a mind or the circumspection of an acute observer but is immanent in practical, perceptual activity (Ingold, 2011: 416). Paterson (2007: 130) describes digital media as "technologies of touch." Richardson (2008) reflects that digital media incorporate the body into their functioning, becoming not an extension of man but an assemblage of man and media. This is akin to Thrift's (1996) "sensuousness of practice" with regards to the body interacting with things in everyday practice. In addition, Hjorth, Wilken and Gu (2012: 56) describe this practice as "ambient intimacy," where the closeness to the device results in a visceral awareness and mode of embodiment that draws together the virtual and actual and the distant and near. The concerns of these theorists are with movement, proximity and, most importantly in this framework, dwelling (being-at-home with technology). Richardson (2012: 135) describes this as "intercorporeality," referring to the irreducible relations between the technology, embodiment, knowledge and perception with the result a socio-technical or techno-corporeal hybrid. Miller (2014: 218) describes the phenomenology of this embodiment with mobile technology as an extension of mediatisation into the lifeworld, and I agree with that conclusion on the kind of relation between the body and device.

The research reported is explicitly concerned with place and the subjective phenomenological feeling of place, however, and in focussing upon this aspect the role of the hand and embodiment (also critical in Farman, 2012, in the Introduction) must be integrated or reconciled with the care, attunement and mood of Dasein that has been argued for previously as key to placehood. Digital technology has contact with the body, and it is in this use by the body that the previously identified taking-into-care is achieved through everyday use.

If one considers how care is achieved through the body it is self-evident that when my own body is considered, including the hand, "I" am surrounded by it; the body is involved in the world, in the here and now, situated and that I am that body. However, "I" am not concerned with the body in a state of average everydayness. I experience my body in antepredicative knowledge (Merleau-Ponty, 2002), in that it is the grounding for my existence in the world but not the focus of my attention of the world. I am aware of parts of my body at different times; if I stub my toe, I am certainly aware of my toe, but normally I am content for the toe not to be perceived at all while safe in the knowledge that it is *my* toe and *my toe* is a part of my body that is me. As such, I do not have an ongoing objective process or form of objective epistemology that informs me of the goings on of my body. The processes of my body, the parts of the body and the body as a unified thing that is situated in the world are all beyond my average, everyday circumspection. One can from this position extrapolate further, however, on the body. As Merleau-Ponty (2002) expresses, the body is the vehicle of our being in the world, and having a body is to be intervolved in the environment. Without the body, we would not be in the world in the way that we understand the world. While I am not conscious of my body in this way, it is the unperceived turning to the world that allows me to know about and inspect objects, orient myself to things and understand the world meaningfully. I do not extricate myself from the body and the elements of me so fond of philosophers – the psychic and the physical, or mind and body – are integrated in their presence in the world that is only possible through the embodiment and situations that the body allows.

As a being with a body, its absence is inconceivable but it is not a thing that is observed. Other bodies and objects are observed, and the body is the means of doing this in the world. One's own body is not perceived in this way, however. However, I am aware of the body in motion, in a way that contact with other things does not make such awareness possible. Take for example the use of a hammer as analysed in Heidegger's (1962) analysis of tool-being. When I use a hammer for hammering nails, the hammer in use withdraws from my conscious awareness or circumspection. While the hammer is being used by me as an embodied entity (in my right hand, in motion through the movement of my right arm) the object itself is not the focus of my attention during the activity. This is the engagement with things that humans have when using ready-to-hand tools. The withdrawal of the thing from the conspicuousness of the embodied human (Dasein in Heidegger's terms, being-there that is not necessarily concerned with embodiment yet still emphasises situatedness in the world) in its use as a tool would contrast to how the tool is viewed when not used. As a present-to-hand object, the type of circumspection is different. The tool can be considered in terms of weight, size, colour, state of repair or any other quality. In use, it withdraws from such circumspection.

Just as for a tool there are different modes of revealing and circumspection, so too there are such ways of seeing with regards to the body. In motion, I am aware of my movement through the world. In being breathless after running, I am aware of the motion of air into and out of my lungs and the soreness of my legs. While I am not conscious of the effects of lactic acid in this effect, nevertheless I am aware and perceive my legs in a way that I do not in rest. This is not my objective body that is hurting, however; this is a phenomenological body that I am experiencing in a particular way. My consciousness of all things, including my own body, is a consciousness of a being-towards-a-thing (the object of consciousness) through the intermediary of the body (Merleau-Ponty, 2002). This holds for my body as well as other things. The body is in a sense the medium for having a world and for having experiences and phenomenal presence that one would call being human, and as care is "the structure of Dasein itself" (Heidegger, 1992: 293), and is existentially is how Dasein is related to the world through its care for the world then the body is vital to care. The taking into care of entities (non-Dasein) requires interaction, and if following Merleau-Ponty the body is the worldly intermediary to interaction, it follows that these bodily interactions with technology are critical to *taking technology into care.*

The conceptualisation of the body as the situating and embodied site of our being-in-the-world is critical to an understanding the relationship between phenomenological being, care and technology. To reiterate, I am not in front of or above my body – I am in it, or more appropriately I am it. I am not a spectator to the machinations of the body, but rather a unifier of the parts of the body into the whole through consciousness. In the context of technology, the body utilises (and has utilised for thousands of years) technology in particular ways to augment and facilitate the body in the world. Take for example eyeglasses. An eyeglass wearer uses this artefact to correct an impediment to the body that is used to perceive and understand the world, but in the wearing of the glasses *is not aware of the wearing.* Glasses recede from circumspection as one uses them in the world, unless they are broken or missing – then one is only too aware of the presence or absence of the device. Ihde (1990) calls this relationship to technology an embodiment relation, in that when using such technology the artefact itself is absorbed into the withdrawing of the body or hand (in the same way that one would not be concerned with the physical characteristics or functions of the eye when looking at something). These embodiment relations are common and everyday – think of the clothes you are wearing as you read this line, and realise that just seconds ago you had no conscious awareness of the same because you were in an embodiment relation with those clothes.

A technology such as a smartphone typically has an embodiment relation, but they may also have a more important, meaningful relation with us. Take the wristwatch. Mumford (1934) claimed that the clock, not the steam engine, was the critical machine in the modern world because of the way that it operates to structure time and human activity in a linear manner in line with the passing of time. Heidegger (1962), in arguing that technologies take account of and reveal nature itself in some way, saw clocks and clock-cultures as having a fundamentally different relation to time compared to non-clock-cultures. Clocks themselves, for Heidegger, enabled an existential temporality where time is divided into discreet partitions for activity and shared and individual praxis. Nature itself is read differently by clocks, however; time by clock allows for a measurability of the processes of nature and therefore a fundamentally different relation to nature through a differentiated understanding. Ihde (1990) terms this relation through technology as a hermeneutic relation, in that understandings of the world are achieved through the engagement with this kind of technology.

The hermeneutic nature of the relations between humans and LBSN should be obvious. Once humans know how to *read* the outputs of the technology, then knowledge of the world is augmented, shaped and changed by that reading. In the case of the clock, the reading of time leads to segmentation of the day, activities being assigned to times and normalisation of social and working practices according to the division of time. LBSN applications stand in hermeneutic relation too; the technology presents something to the person (i.e. location, places and social gazetteers) and the person will adjust or amend their orientation to place according to the representation of these elements.

If that was all the technology was responsible for, then the analysis could be concluded here. However, LBSNs are also not like a wristwatch or clock. A wristwatch represents time to the wearer; LBSN *stores and shares* information on places and retrieves information that is semantically and algorithmically relevant due to the functioning of code. This shift is radical because while the technology has both an embodiment and hermeneutic relation with the user, it also has an alterity and opacity that makes this kind of technology problematic when considering its role in human affairs. The technology, in executing code, is not open to scrutiny. Harman's analysis of Heidegger's notion of *Zeug* or equipment leads to the conclusion that equipment is always in reality but withdrawn in order to be ready-to-hand (Harman, 2002: 22). Objects are withdrawn in the sense that their "being" is not fully revealed in use, but humans and other things still operate in the world seemingly unaware of or unconcerned about this withdrawal through the presence of the sensual element. In our everydayness, we do not stop to consider the ontological status of the tool that we are using (except perhaps when present-at-hand) and use the tool beyond the conspicuousness of consciousness. This is the 'vicarious causation' (Berry, 2011: 153) that encapsulates the way the world is presented through devices; the means of understanding the world (from the referential totality) is necessarily vicarious through the way that those devices are continually emerging and withdrawing into the clearing of understanding that is the referential totality, due to the computational device (the wearable technology in this case) itself having an internal hidden state through code.

In short, the device (while involved with the user in embodied and hermeneutic relations) functions in a way that renders a truth to the phenomenological and habitual experience of the world. It is necessary to understand how the device is responsible for the representational framework for the user and how such a framework is constructed from a number of distinct interoperating parts into a device which nonetheless operates in a form that can be said to be radically opaque, whilst also being *unready-to-hand* (Berry, 2011: 126) as the sum of the parts of the device are conspicuousness in functioning. The way-of-being inaugurated by equipment (the computational devices) is a way-of-being that is dependent on a computational device that has an internal hidden state. That hidden state is the functioning of the components through the execution of code. As part of the functioning of computational devices, this dual aspect of invisibility (of the underlying computational processes) combined with the feedback and representations of place from databanks and databases comports the user towards a new understanding of place. This happens while the embodied actions of use and the tool being used are withdrawn from circumspection, as the embodiment of the device becomes, as Richardson (2012: 135) argues, "intercorporeal" in the irreducible relation between technology, embodiment, knowledge, perception and understanding of the world. A new understanding or comportment to self therefore arises from the combination of embodiment, hermeneutic relations and the radical alterity of the technology. In embodiment, we are attuned to the device and the device in turn attunes to the world; the question is therefore: what does the proliferation of software, devices, code and data mean for the world?

Alterity and the digital world

To recap, Heidegger's notion of care is critical to understanding how we make sense of place. Care is a function of mood, that is the towards-which or orientation to things. The mood can lead to the possibility of a technological or poetic revealing of place (the later being place as *place*, an existential locale based on the referential totality of the things in that place). The world revealing itself necessitates the taking into care *of something* – in this case the computational device and LBSN. This is achieved through a relationship between the thing and the body, and the thing relates to the user through the embodied (practices, physical interactions) relations, hermeneutic relations (the meanings of the world presented to the user) and importantly an alterity relation where the functioning of code is withdrawn from the user. It is the final relation that requires further attention: what role does code play in the appreciation of place given its removal from our circumspection. Essentially, this questions how the device and embodied being-there is linked to the data- and information-infused world and therefore how code is critical to attuning to this world and understanding place in the digital age.

To position code in this post-phenomenology, an additional element is needed in this framework that explains the position of man in the digital world and how code assists in dwelling through its functioning. Sloterdijk's *Spharen* project can be seen as a trilogy of works that answers the question "where is man?" rather than "what is man?" (Schinkel and Noordegraaf-Eelens, 2011: 11), as an engagement in a Heideggerian project concerning the nature of being in relation to place rather than time (Elden and Mendieta, 2009: 6). Like Heidegger, Sloterdijk makes much of the thrownness of man into the world, through the negative gynaecology (Sloterdijk, 1998: 275) of being cast from the womb into the world. This thrownness or not being comfortable in the world makes man a restless creature that is always remaking worlds, fashioning dwellings and dwelling as a phenomenological being in the world through connection with the Other (Elden and Mendieta, 2009: 7). Essentially, man is always looking to normalise its spatial existence and find comfort (van Tuinen, 2009: 299). The project establishes being-in-the-world as being-in-spheres, in that being is always spatial and social (in that it is always being-with). The concept of the sphere refers to the "Da-" of Heidegger's Dasein in that it refers to "there," man being in spaces that are opened up by presence and which are given form, substance, extension, duration and meaning by man "being-there." For Sloterdijk, spheres are "the original product of human being-together," in other words shared spaces of perception and experience. Sloterdijk's project moves from micro-spheres (or bubbles) which are the most intimate spheres of co-existence, such as the intra-uteral relationship between unborn child and mother, to the macro-sphere level of globes and to the globalised level of foam. It is the last type of spherical relationship, foam, that is of interest when considering the worlding of humans using code, but an understanding of this is dependent upon an understanding of the levels of sphere that precede this as the development of the globalised foam is contingent on and resultant from the development of other spheres in human history.

A sphere is a shared psycho-spatial immunological edifice (Schinkel and Noordegraaf-Eelens, 2011: 13). In simpler terms, a sphere is a shared, lived-in space and a way to conceptualise social life as consisting of the continual building up and leaving of spatial connectives, from the basic dyad to the complex swarm of people. Sloterdijk's historical project traces the development of these spheres from the micro-level of the interpersonal, to the macro-level of the globe and terrestrial conquest, to the multiplicity of simultaneous connections that overcome spatial and temporal barriers in the globalised, "foam" sphere. The "where" conceptualised is a protective sphere that can be virtual, but is nevertheless always meaningful and reassuring as a place distinguished from the infinite and fragmentary world (Schinkel and Noordegraaf-Eelens, 2011: 22). This spherical topos draws attention to where people live, act, practice their everyday habits and activities and indeed *are*. This is never a static place, with self-defining borders and measures, nor is it static place in the sense of being boundless and without measure – it is a dynamic, changing place where one moves from sphere to sphere as the meaning and intention of life changes. Societies themselves consist of these "turbulent and asymmetrical associations of space-multiplicities" or spheres (Sloterdijk, 2004: 57).

The spheres are therefore what being-in-the-world structurally is, in that the sphere is *being-with*. Elden (2012: 8) reiterates that the spheres of being-with come in different sizes, from the dyadic bubbles (microspherology), to globes (macro-spherology) and the plural-spherology (a multitude of bubbles connecting and reconnecting) of the foam. The latter is "an interlocking and multiple set of cells" that are representative of connection and relation. Klausner (in Elden, 2012: 8) identifies four attributes of foam: it is made up of variable shapes and sizes; it lacks a clear centre; it is both fragile and interconnected; and it is part of a process of creation. Foam, then, is a metaphorical attempt to conceptualise the ever-changing places of being-in-the-world, from the smaller and more intimate to the networked and globalised. Foam is not centred on the person; it is a place that is characterised by particular connections, or being-with. These connections are not just fragile in that they are non-permanent, but necessarily fragile as the sphere is creative and old connections (and therefore old bubbles) are constantly being replaced by the new in foam. Elden (2012: 8) rightly draws parallels between this view and Deleuze and Guattari's concept of the rhizome, but, unlike the rhizome, foams are loosely structured and not reducible to complex arrangements and networks. Foams are made of bubbles that are connected but always separate. Sloterdijk's bubbles therefore enter a process of osmotic integration with other bubbles, and this multitude of bubbles (enabled by networked communications as well as physical proximity) makes up the foam. Importantly, the bubbles are both connected and isolated. This kind of vicarious connection indicates that while the bubble is connected to others it is not reducible to its connections, and therefore is not just a node brought into being by virtue of a network of connections and extinguished accordingly at the dissolution of that network.

The *mit-sein* that is a bubble is always being-among-others, a kind of dwelling and always a dwelling among others. Like Heidegger's concept of dwelling as a freedom from the world of *Das Man* and a technologically enframed mode of being, Sloterdijk's dwelling is a worlding and bringing-forth of the world rather than a standing-forth or *Bestand* that is forced upon man. As Morin (2009: 58) argues, this is an attempt to theorise contemporary society through a reworking of Heidegger's existential analytic of Dasein, and draws on a detailed narrative of the historical development of humankind and human society to reach this aim. Sloterdijk interprets the development of humanity as a development of different forms of spatiality and different ways of understanding and using space. The move from micro-sphere to plural-sphere is a move that is from strong, close relationship to weaker, looser ties facilitated by the technological milieu that allows for such ties to exist. The stage of foam is contingent upon the micro-spheres of bubbles and macro-spheres of globes (representations of the global as an ontological and epistemological attempt to normalise and conceptualise space through homogenisation) and deliberately goes beyond Heidegger's own analysis of technology as *Gestell* or standing reserve. Indeed, that analysis is akin to the second phase of spheres, the globes or terrestrial globalisation as a worldview based on the positioning of the world as a resource to be used. The third phase of foam addresses the modern thinking and calculative assessment associated with networked society (Morin, 2009: 59).

In order to understand the relevance of Sloterdijk to understanding place through LBSN, it is necessary to trace what kinds of world-forming praxis "global foams" allow to be conceived (Morin, 2009: 60). Foams are processes that lend themselves to stability and inclusiveness (Sloterdijk, 2004: 50). With regards to the social, the basic component of the social is the dyadic sphere, and the social itself is composed of inter-subjective relations between autonomous subjects. The human never exists alone, but only in the world of co-subjectivity where the human is animated by the presence and gaze of others (Laermans, 2011: 115). The social is effectively a product of the reality where humans only share the walls that separate well-equipped "ego-spheres" from one another (Sloterdijk, 2004: 501). The possibility and realisation of this co-existence is possible through the communication networks that link people to known and unknown others (Laermans, 2011: 116). Contemporary individualism in the age of social media is a twist to co-existence. The individual splits itself into an actual self and a virtual or potential self which results in an endless internal dialogue between these two selves as well as connections to others (Laermans, 2011: 116). Society itself is conceived as aggregate of microspheres (Sloterdijk, 2004: 59) where each bubble is a "world," an intimate space that has its own importance and significance. Each world is simultaneously linked to all other worlds, but also separated by flexible boundaries that create an overall situation of co-existence and co-isolation (Sloterdijk, 2004: 255). The whole is not independent of the smaller parts, but the worldview given here is unstable and chaotic (ten Bos, 2009: 85), where a comfortable existence is always threatened and needs to be remade through new connections, as connections between bubbles change continually affecting the foam.

With regards to everyday praxis, one can consider the use of media and computational devices as praxes of world-making and sphere-creation. Traditional broadcast media produce a constantly renewed and fleeting cohesion-effect through the production of common news themes and common interests (Laermans, 2011: 117). Mass media communications arouse temporary interests that produce an affective involvement in the topic, and which are therefore responsible for the construction of spheres. Thus, media produces instant cohesion through a bombarding of the "foam" bubbles that make up contemporary society (Laermans, 2011: 118). This mass media information is not stored, but simultaneously produced and used up in its reception, and while there is a surplus of information in modern society there is still a process of making and reproducing to attract and sustain attention (Laermans, 2011: 120).

The mass media had power through the centralised position and ability to synchronise the attention of many individuals and other "ego-spheres" (Laermans, 2011: 126), thus creating a common sphere of interest or attention. However, the digital and social media environment lacks this cohesion. Merrin (2014: 2) contextualises the presence of digital computational devices or gadgets within a rise of hyper-ludic media – hyperfunctional gadgets that are closely related to "me-dia" (media streams and production centred on the individual) and away from traditional broadcast media. This kind of media therefore allows for a highly personal media experience that is dependent on the execution of code and contributes to the subjective experience of the world of the user. When considering social media and the devices used to connect to these platforms, the common sphere is the medium, but the messages on platforms such as Twitter are more numerous, diverse, personalised and fragmentary than on any broadcast medium and reliant on code to function. In a society that is saturated with mediation, messages and people are left fishing for attention in an attention economy and media landscape. In considering the impact of social media and LBSN specifically it is the notion of attentiveness or mindfulness that is critical. The media messages (posts, tips, tweets) that create attention in the user create a "bubble" of attention from the foam of countless media messages carried through digital media. In this praxis of social media use as a worlding, place and location are a determiner of attention that allows for the reception and engaging with particular media messages provided by other users. Hence, LBSN harnesses social gazetteers, location information and personally relevant data for users through the execution of code in a place to present the world in a particular form.

So, in a place where networked connectivity is possible, the feeling of place can be achieved through the use of applications that inform on place: giving information, relative location and cues and information from others that provide a social dimension to the praxis (a being-with or bubble). Code, in this view, acts as a membrane that allows for flows of data, information and social activity through the foam and into bubbles. Code is the membrane that allows for the information that characterises the networked society to flow and influence. The presence of code therefore foregrounds our presence in modern world, affording the possibilities of dwelling and understanding while being withdrawn and opaque to the users of computational devices. Code links foam and bubble and the understanding of the modern world is inexorably linked to its presence. As such, code plays the critical role in worlding in the information-infused world; we attune to the world through embodied interactions with code through our devices.

Mobile computational devices and connectivity create place

In conclusion, smartphones within particular contexts project a processual agency of computational code (Berry, 2011: 28). The construction of the device involves a series of individual parts that operate in unison through the execution of computational code as part of a process that allows for the revealing of place. This is additionally dependent upon the mood of the user, the practices of use and the particular relations with the device and the environment as an atmosphere of digital connectivity.

The way-of-being inaugurated by equipment (the computational devices) that affects the phenomenological experience of place, in which the user is coping through a continual computational mapping (Kitchin et al., 2012) and will-to-map that the computational device allows and facilitates, is a way-of-being that is dependent on a computational device that has an internal hidden state. That hidden state is the functioning of the components through the execution of code, and so to understand "thinging" at the material level, i.e. how the device is a thing, the parts of the device and the code of LBSN need to be considered with regards to how they function and how this functioning facilitates the poetic revealing of place. It is also important to note that this unreadiness-to-hand creates tensions for the user both in assisting in locating and *identifying* place, and also in fragmenting and deterritorialising place. Berry explains:

> This is the phenomena of "unreadiness-to-hand" which forces us to re-focus on the equipment, because it frustrates any activity temporarily (Blattner 2006: 58), that is that the situation requires deliberate attention ... Conspicuousness, then, "presents the available equipment as in a certain unavailableness" (Heidegger, 1978: 102–103), so that as Dreyfus (2001a: 71) explains, we are momentarily startled, and then shift to a new way of coping, but which, if help is given quickly or the situation is resolved, then "transparent circumspective behaviour can be so quickly and easily restored that no new stance on the part of Dasein is required" (Dreyfus, 2001a: 72). As Heidegger puts it, it requires "a more precise kind of circumspection, such as 'inspecting', checking up on what has been attained, [etc.]" (Dreyfus, 2001a: 70). (Berry, 2011: 126)

In other words, as part of the functioning of computational devices, this dual aspect of invisibility (of the underlying computational processes) combined with the pressing call to the user to interact (from the user interface) places the user within the context of the identified "gathered" code/space (Dodge and Kitchin, 2004) whilst calling them into the "place" or interface of the mobile device. They argue:

> Our premise is that as people traverse space, individual mobilities, interactions and transactions in combination with code beckon particular forms of space into being. Here, we conceive of space as a form of ontogenesis (always coming into being); space as practice; as a doing; as an event (rather than an absolute, geometric abstraction or simply a social construction; see Hubbard et al., 2002) ... we feel it is more profitable to think of the on-going production of space as one of transduction – in which performativity is one component,

but which also recognises the salience of objects and non-humans. (Dodge and Kitchin, 2004: 4–5)

This is a useful way to think about place, too, as interactions with technology reveal aspects of the technology (while other aspects remain withdrawn) and reveal the world in a particular manner according to the comportment of the user to that technology as technology is a mode of revealing (in Malpas and Wrathall, 2000: 206).

This analysis positions *code as the level of computation that allows for a surfacing or making visible of place*. Code functions to draw together the requisite elements in an understanding of place in the digital world: user, information and data, device, environment and the feeling of place. Following the discussion of Heidegger's fourfold earlier in this chapter, one can map these onto Heidegger's own elements: *mortals* as user (disposed or oriented in a particular manner); *gods/divinities* as the feeling of place; *skies* as the information and data returned about place by the device; and *earth* as the embodied practices of use in a digitally-infused environment. Code is positioned as the membrane that allows movement phenomenologically to a sense of place. Code gathers and surfaces the requisite elements to understand place; code is accessed through embodied practices and hermeneutically orders information to understand place if that user is in mood or orientation to place; and code allows access to the "foaming" environment of digital information.

To complete this discussion, the code of Foursquare can be briefly considered and analysed in the context of how it achieves this multi-faceted gathering. For the purposes of this discussion a functional account of computation is used to describe the computation of the mobile computational device. Fresco (2010: 166–171) summarises three views of what computation is: the semantic view, the causal view and the functional view. The semantic view is summarised by Fodor (1981: 122) as "computation is a causal chain of computer states and the links in the chain are operations on semantically interpreted formulas in a machine code ... there is no computation without representation." Theorists that hold this view (Fodor, 1981; Pylyshyn, 1989; Smith, 1996) attribute semantic properties to internal computations in a computer, and so maintain that computation is a symbolic phenomenon (Fresco, 2010: 167). Proponents of the causal view (Chalmers, 1994; Copeland, 1996; Scheutz, 1999) hold that computation is best explained without recourse to semantic properties and instead is a function of the causal properties of the process itself (Fresco, 2010: 169). Chalmers (1994: 391–393) argues the crucial link between abstract computation and physical mechanisms is a theory of implementation, and thus it is implementation that is the relation between computation and physical machine. Computation is the implementation of a set of physical states (in the device) mapped to a one-to-one relation to the abstract computational state, and therefore computation is a product of causal organisation (Fresco, 2010: 169). Thirdly, the functional view (Popper and Eccles, 2006; Piccinini, 2007) claims that a computational device has components, which have functions and are organised in a certain way – the mechanism's capabilities are constituted by the organisation of the components. Therefore its functioning state is how computation is realised (Fresco, 2010: 171).

A semantic account is rejected here, as internal semantics are difficult to substantiate in a phenomenological account of the world.[6] The causal account is also rejected, as this account does not afford importance to components and additions to devices, as well as omitting the role of a user in the computational process, which would be at odds with my hypotheses for this thesis. By using the functional account, mobile computational devices are conceptualised as computational in that they have assembled different components (assisted-GPS unit, silicon compass, accelerometers, gyroscopes) to produce a particular computation but also a computational state itself, that is: computation is a product of the material units that enable computation.

Computation is the running of code and therefore the operations of the device; following Dodge and Kitchin (2004), this creates not just code/space but also *code/place*, where an embodied user in a particular mood uses the device to understand place in the digital environment. Here, just two examples of Foursquare code (in JavaScript) are used to illustrate how the code of LBSN gathers to allow a revealing of place.

The code of the application illustrates how this functional computation is realised by the software calling a Foursquare API to locate the device and user (Figure 4.2). By drawing on elements in the device and by networking with other devices, the code draws together information that "assembles the location" for the user. The key components of the device itself (a-GPS unit, digital clock, 3G sim card or Wi-Fi connection unit) are augmented by connection with information held by the company and with other computational devices (satellite, Internet relay provider, Wi-Fi router) to create a series of connections that allow the location to be ascertained in real time. In this, there is a method of locating oneself and one's device mediated by the device and its associations. While the idea of the ordering is problematic in that the technological mode of revealing is in itself an ordering that reveals as

```
{
    checkins:[
        {
            id:286939,
            user:{
                id:467,
                firstname:'S****',
                lastname:'S******',
                photo:'http://foursquare.com/userpix/
                467_1237171998.jpg',
                gender:'female'
            },
            venue:{
                id:44379,
                name:'Topshop',
                address:'478 Broadway',
                crossstreet:'at Broome',
                geolat:40.7215,
                geolong:-74.0001
            },
            distance:2382,
            display:'Sarah S. @ Topshop',
            shout:'Just tried on a dress ...',
            created:'Thu, 21 May 09 18:09:22 +0000'
        }
    ]
}
```

Figure 4.2 Foursquare check-in code
Source: Foursquare Developers Blog, 2011.

resource, one can see that code is a gathering – whether the mood of the user is towards a revealing of place or not.

The code draws information together from the device to create a check-in to a specific location. Initially the device assembles information on the user from the Foursquare database: the identification number, name, photograph URL and gender. This information is a symbolic representation of the act of checking-in with regards to the person that is acting to use the device and LBSN – a gathering of the person (or mortal, to use the term Heidegger ascribed). The information on the venue, extracted from a database, is itself part of the code – the name of the place and address, created by a user previous to this one with the geo-locational data provided by the a-GPS unit, the latitudinal and longitudinal data that is provided by that component to locate the device.[7] In this part of the check-in, the GPS unit of the iPhone operates in co-ordination with four or more of the 24 satellites[8] in orbit as part of the Global Positioning System to determine the location of the user and device. The "call" of the user, for that is in effect what the user is doing at that place at that time, is displayed as inputted at check-in and then held in the database for other users to see at subsequent check-ins.[9] This social aspect of the activity is shared with other users and can be used as a source of information on the venue by future users. Finally, the time of the check-in is another element assembled by the device. This timestamp is both given by the device and checked by the GPS satellites, which the a-GPS unit in the phone connects with to ascertain the location of the device on earth. This user has made a simple check-in to Foursquare, of visiting Topshop and trying on a dress. The code acts as part of the event, and inscribes the event in a database. The event itself becomes a social gazetteer for the user and other users when shared and stored. The use of the LBSN at that time is also indicative of a *towards-which* from the user to the event that is to share and inscribe the event for others, and this deliberation and consideration for the place, activity and audience is important to consider if one is to argue for the idea that the device and LBSN "thing."

Foursquare code in this instance inscribes the presence and activity of a person at a place at a particular time. The application must encode places for this to happen, and in doing this the application both allows for the revealing of a place as a place and the privileging of places in the database and code over un-coded places "outside" of the application.

Here, place is made stable through its inscription in the application database, and through this exploring of the code one can historically assess the place through the gathering of place by the code (Figure 4.3). In this example, one can determine the location of the place and the nature or function of that place (a park in this instance, as categorised in the database) and also assess how many people have checked-in to the place on the service, how many tips have been left at the place and how many friends on one's friends list have visited the park, etc.

The method of encoding the place in the Foursquare database organises that place in a manner that allows for a revealing of place that is more than simple binary representation of present/absent resource; the location is encoded along with social aspects of the venue that are encouraged and allowed for by the application, and stored historically

```
                                                    ]
    }
    venue: {
            id: "430d0a00f964a5203e271fe3"
            name: "Brooklyn Bridge Park"
            contact: {
            phone: "+12128033822"
            formattedPhone: "+1 212-803-3822"
            twitter: "bbpconservancy"
    }
            location: {
            address: "Main St."
            crossStreet: "Plymouth St."
            lat: 40.701593743002
            lng: -73.99592399597168
            distance: 387
            postalCode: "11201"
            city: "Brooklyn"
            state: "NY"
            country: "United States"
     }
            categories: [
              {
                id: "4bf58dd8d48988d163941735"
                name: "Park"
                 pluralName: "Parks"
                shortName: "Park"
            icon: {
                prefix: "https://foursquare.com/img/
            categories/parks_outdoors/default_"
                sizes: [
                              32
                              44
                              64
                              88
                              256
            ]
            name: ".png"
```

Figure 4.3 Data code for Brooklyn Bridge Park on Foursquare
Source: Foursquare Developers Blog, 2011.

```
              }
              primary: true
              }
      ]
              verified: true
              stats: {
              checkinsCount: 9498
              usersCount: 5959
              tipCount: 64
              photoCount: 217
      }
                specials: {
                count: 0
                items: [ ]
      }
              hereNow: {
              count: 0
      }
              beenHere: {
              count: 0
              marked: false
        }
              friendVisits: {
              count: 3
              items: [
  {
```

Figure 4.3 Continued

as data that can be accessed by other users to familiarise themselves with the place and bring a historical context forth about that place. The computational device surfaces place through organising the information in a manner that allows place (as a meaningful locale) rather than space (as co-ordinate) to come forward.

Code and post-phenomenology

Code has been positioned as the key element in the revealing of place by LBSN in this analysis. One might, after reading this account, question why an entire chapter of this book was dedicated to the Heideggerian analysis of care as critical to phenomenological place in the previous chapter. The *digital post-phenomenology* that encompasses bodily relations, hermeneutic relations and alterity relations within an environment of data and information that is accessed contingently on the functioning of code appears to supersede the initial Heideggerian contribution. However, as will become clear, the orientation or mood of the situated being that is the human user is critical to the understanding of place that arises through the use of LBSN. Indeed, this understanding is still drawn along the technological and poetic/dwelling distinction outlined in the Heidegger exegesis.

The extension of Heidegger's phenomenology in this chapter – the accessing of coded devices through the body, the taking of the device into care through the body and the body situated in a software- and data-infused environment which is attuned to through use – is necessary in both contemporising the phenomenology into a post-phenomenology and giving adequate consideration to how we move and live in the digital world. Sloterdijk's notion of a bubble in the foam includes the notion of being-there in a mood, the body as the vehicle for that being-there, the device as part of the sphere and the presence of information and data as the foam in which bubbles are constantly making, breaking and remaking connections and creating the "social." The resulting "bubbles" where connections have augmented, altered or added to experience of the world are the phenomenological experience of being in the world. In this, code takes the role of the membrane that allows for these connections.

However, as the following two chapters will illustrate, the phenomenological experience of place is by no means set; code allows for this digital post-phenomenology of place to *happen*, but the mood of the user is critical to *how this is experienced*.

5
Sharing Location with Locative Social Media

To understand the use of LBSN in everyday contexts and how this affects users' experience of place, a substantial and original body of research on user experiences needed to the conducted. This chapter will detail he methods and techniques used in that research process, and will detail the practices and behaviours of using LBSN that are indicative of a deep understanding of place as a meaningful existential locale.

Method – Ethnography of LBSN users

The research detailed here is an ethnography of users of the LBSN Foursquare. While there were numerous other LBSNs available in 2011 (such as Gowalla, BrightKite, Rally Up and Yelp!), Foursquare had distinct advantages as a research site. Firstly, with ten million users as of June 2011 (Foursquare, 2011), there were obviously a large number of potential participants using the Foursquare service, especially in comparison to other LBSNs. Secondly, the architecture of the Foursquare service was beneficial to the type of research being carried out. The service allows users to contact other users that they are "friends" with via email, Twitter, Facebook and comments, so the ability to reach other users was superior to other platforms available.

Given the single site of research, this project is, in effect, a critical case study of Foursquare users. Given that Foursquare is dependent upon using an Internet-enabled smartphone, the critical case study is from the technological perspective of smartphone (or computational device) users. There are obviously some issues with the validity of this method; case studies are perceived as problematic for the reasons Flyvbjerg (2006: 219) lists: one cannot generalise from a single case, therefore case studies cannot contribute to scientific knowledge; case studies are only useful for generating hypotheses, not testing hypotheses; the case study method is biased towards verification and there is difficulty in summarising specific case studies. Flyvbjerg dismisses these traditional criticisms of the method: one can often generalise on the basis of a single case, and the case study may be central to scientific development via generalisation as supplement or alternative to other methods. Formal generalisation itself is overvalued as a source of scientific development, whereas "the force of example" is underestimated (Flyvbjerg, 2006: 228). With regards to the answering of hypotheses, it is impossible to assess pre-research whether a case will be paradigmatic in the sense of addressing major hypotheses, or whether it will generate further research questions (Flyvbjerg, 2006: 233). Flyvbjerg argues that the case study contains no greater bias toward verification of the researcher's preconceived notions than other methods of inquiry; on the contrary, experience indicates that the case study contains a greater bias toward falsification of preconceived notions than toward verification (2006: 237). Any problems in summarising case studies are more often due to the properties of the reality studied than to the case study as a research method. Often, it is not desirable to summarise and generalise case studies and good studies should be read as narratives in their entirety (2006: 240–241).

In particular, Flyvbjerg (2006: 241) argues that such conventional wisdom on case studies is a necessary and sufficient method for certain research tasks. Arguing about the research climate in the social sciences, Flyvbjerg notes that good social science is problem-driven rather than method-driven, and citing Kuhn (1987) reiterates that "a discipline without a large number of thoroughly executed case studies is a discipline without systematic production of exemplars, and that a discipline without exemplars is an ineffective one." In defence of this research, the use of the case study method is in response to the problem being investigated rather than a methodological preference. The need to study a group of users that are engaged with a LBSN that remediates place, with a view to conducting in-depth research that would derive appropriate detailed responses for the phenomenological focus of the research questions, meant a case study of Foursquare users was an appropriate method of research in this context.

The term ethnography may be loosely applied to any qualitative research project where the purpose is to provide a detailed, in-depth description of everyday life and practice – such as this research on the use of LBSN in everyday life. Ethnography is defined as both a qualitative research process and method (one *conducts* an ethnography) and product (the *outcome* of this process is an ethnography) whose aim is cultural interpretation (Geertz, 1973: 3). van Maanen (1997: 3) states that ethnography is "the written representation of culture." The ethnography in this research took the form of a virtual ethnography. Virtual ethnography involves using a different set of tools for the collection of data from a traditional ethnography. While an anthropological ethnography that occurs "in real life" is conducted to detail the experiences of people in specific cultural milieu, a virtual ethnography will look to do the same in an environment that lends itself to different means of collection of data. As the LBSN Foursquare is either a web-based application or one accessed via an internet-enabled mobile device (phone, tablet computer) then the virtual ethnography is appropriate here, given that action and use of the LBSN is situated in the virtual environment as well as the physical environment.

An obvious criticism of this is that there are not as many face-to-face or traditional embedded ethnographic methods (identified as critical by, amongst others, Boellstorff et al., 2012). There are two points of reply to such a criticism. Firstly, as users are contactable through the virtual route, this makes sustained contact easier. Secondly, as the user base of Foursquare is global rather than local, and uptake of the service varies across geographical area then to obtain a representative sample of users, it was decided to use virtual methods that effectively overcome issues of geographical uptake of the service. The virtual ethnography can utilise a number of computer-based methods of data collection in order to collect the data that can be used in the construction of the ethnographic profile of a community.

Participant observation still remains the critical element of the ethnographic process (Boellstorff et al., 2012: 65), but the role of the researcher is somewhat different to the traditional anthropological ethnographic role. According to Miller and Slater (2001: 21–22), the immersion in a particular case, the reference to a specific locality and participant observation are still the cornerstones of ethnographic research, even when using the Internet as the research environment. However, the notion of the field itself is radically altered, since the field is now a group of people involved in using an application scattered worldwide in physical geography. For this reason, the virtual ethnography was appealing for this research as it allowed for a wide range of participants (geographically) to be sampled while still allowing for an effective ethnographic method to be applied. To engage in participant observation in this case, the researcher not only interviewed participants but also followed them on Foursquare: investigating the other participants' behaviours (and corroborating their responses in the process) and using the LBSN to gain insights as a participant and a researcher. While participant observation is different to the physically embedded observation of traditional research, it was critical to understanding the social networking that was part of the research.

While this seems an unconventional ethnographic method, the methods and techniques of conducting ethnographic research in virtual or online environments are far from standard.[1] In lieu of a uniform method, Hine (2000: 66–71) produced a methodological framework for the construction of virtual ethnographic research. Hine identifies the following as critical features of virtual ethnography: the ethnography of mediated interaction often asks researchers to be mobile both virtually and physically; virtual ethnography is a process of intermittent engagement, rather than long-term immersion; virtual ethnography is necessarily partial. Accounts can be based on strategic relevance to particular research questions, rather than faithful representations of objective realities; and virtual ethnography is ultimately an adaptive ethnography which sets out to suit itself to the conditions in which it finds itself. In this study, the contention that virtual ethnography is a process of intermittent engagement, rather than long-term immersion, is important. This indicates a greater flexibility in the ethnographic process. An obvious criticism is that virtual ethnography will not have sufficient breadth of coverage to make significant points about behaviour of online actors; but this is a criticism that can be levelled at any number of research methodologies throughout the social sciences. What is advantageous in this case is that there is the possibility of breadth. Ethnographies rooted in one community will have depth of information on that community, but will be hindered by the fact that it is only a singular community that is being studied. A virtual ethnography may encompass some degree of breadth of communities without sacrificing the depth of study that is a defining characteristic of the ethnographic method.

The data for the ethnography was collected using two methods: a qualitative survey used to discover reasons for using LBSN from users and in-depth interviews that address the primary phenomenological concerns of this thesis. The qualitative survey was done from October 2010 to November 2010. The survey was based online, on the site Surveymonkey.com.[2] 43 participants took part in the survey (from seven countries), with the sample being comprised of 13 females and 30 males; 12 participants were in the 16–25 age range, 11 in the 26–35 range, 11 in the 36–45 range, seven in the 46–55 range and two participants chose not to disclose their age. The participants were sampled using opportunity sampling. During August and September 2010, I added as many Foursquare users as possible to my friends list on the service. By 21 September, I had 241 "friends" on the LBSN. I then emailed every "friend" that had email as a contact option (n = 161) with a request to take part in the survey. From these 161 emails, 43 people completed the survey. The sample is therefore recognised as biased in that the users sampled were not just users, but users interested in the LBSN. However, as this survey is part of a case study it is not argued to be representational of anything but users of the LBSN. As all the participants were connected to my Foursquare profile, I was able to collect the relevant demographic information (age, gender, location) from each profile. Again, participants were not given an opportunity to offer any personal information that would allow them to be identified, unless they offered their email address in order to be asked further questions on the topic. 35 participants provided their email addresses to be contacted about being interviewed in the next stage of the research, although only seven of those participants agreed to interviews once contacted.

The survey consisted of nine questions; question one being a request for an email address, and question nine asking if participants would agree to be contacted with further questions. Question two asked about the type of device participants used to access Foursquare. Questions three to eight were open-ended questions asking participants to reflect upon why they began using the LBSN, why they used it in everyday life and continued to use it, and how using the LBSN had affected the way the participants considered the places around them and their relationships with other friends.

Following the surveys, 32 interviews were conducted, all with Foursquare users that were recruited using three techniques. Firstly, a set of interviewees (n=7) was taken from the sample of survey respondents for the qualitative research survey. Secondly, through a message on the Foursquare "Superuser" forum (aboutfoursquare.com), 14 interviewees were sampled. It was decided to use this forum as its users are made up of Foursquare users that have been granted "Superuser" status,[3] and so was seen as an opportune way of recruiting regular users of the service. Thirdly, 13 social media bloggers and commentators were sampled by visiting social media blogs and websites and requesting interviews. This was done to obtain both the reflections of another set of regular users, and, moreover, the reflections of users that had commented and reflected upon their own usage of Foursquare through blogs or articles previously. Again, this is not a representative sample, but these users were specifically selected as frequent users, and as users with significant interest in the LBSN.

The interview itself took three separate forms. Due to the geographically dispersed nature of the sample, interviews were conducted using email. Anders (2000, in Mann and Stewart, 2000: 50; 77) argues that the use of email allows respondents to shape questioning over time, and of course assists the researcher as all interview data is received "auto-transcribed" in textual form. Participants could choose whether to conduct the interview as a series of emails between the interviewee and myself, or to be interviewed via the Skype platform. Each participant in the ethnography was allocated a code to make his or her data anonymous. The second letter of the code indicates whether the participant completed the survey (S), email interview (E), Skype interview (P) or completed a Microsoft Word document with the questions pre-typed into the document (W) – which covers the researcher, who completed the interview questions in a long-form and analysed that data along with the other participants' data. The interview questions were, as in the qualitative survey, open-ended questions, but specifically, the interview questions were written to address the phenomenological experience of using the LBSN Foursquare and the effects of use on the participants' perceptions of space, place and their relationship with technology.

As this research is a phenomenological examination of how experience of place is affected by the use of mobile computational devices and LBSN, the research methods must maintain the character of phenomenology. As a theoretical position, phenomenology argues that the fundamental ontology is consciousness and therefore a phenomenological account must seek to have conscious experience of the world as its central theme. The main focus of phenomenological inquiry is the description of lived experience, and a description of the phenomena as they present themselves or as they are given in experience (Adams, 2010: 2). Phenomenology is investigated in its pre-reflective or pre-verbal immediacy. Conscious experience is not something easily captured; therefore the imperative in the research is to *describe* the conscious experience of participants using LBSN.

The textual analytic method of hermeneutic phenomenological methodology (van Manen, 1997) was used in analysing the data to retain this character. Hermeneutic phenomenological analysis is a "research methodology aimed at producing rich textual descriptions of the experiencing of selected phenomena in the lifeworld of individuals that are able to connect with the experience of all of us collectively" (Smith, 1997: 80). The methods that are inclusive to this approach are thematic analysis, linguistic interpretations, and the honing of exemplary or anecdotal narratives (Adams, 2010: 2). Hermeneutic phenomenological analysis (as a form of textual analysis) is a kind of discourse analysis that is most closely aligned with critical discourse analysis (Fairclough, 1995). Discourse analysis itself is a non-homogeneous technique, and lacks a uniform method; the non-uniformity of the method allows for some creativity in the application of the method. The aspect of discourse in discourse analysis is the emphasis on textual analysis (Jorgensen and Philips, 2002: 61), but this textual analysis avoids a structuralist or formalist approach to the language being analysed, and instead takes a post-structuralist approach to language. This post-structuralism emphasises meaning and the "doing" of things in language, rather than the structural form, and links these semantic features to the context in which the language is used (Richardson, 2002: 22). In the context of this work, the utterances and replies to questions from participants in the ethnography are not to be analysed in the context of what lexical choices are made (or the frequency of lexical choices, as in a content analysis), but instead the focus of the analysis is on drawing out the meaningful and relevant language that relates to the key concerns of the research that have been built on the foundation of phenomenological theory. As such, this is a critical discourse analysis in that the analysis is not neutral in approach. A critical discourse analysis sees language as socially produced and shaping the society in which the language occurs (Fairclough, 1995: 55); the hermeneutic phenomenological analysis treats language as an indicator and reflection of the phenomenological experience of being in the context in which the language is expressing the experience of being in the world in a particular manner rather than the ideological effects of discourse.

To align this analysis closely with phenomenological theory, the themes identified as relevant through the macro-analysis were behaviour, dependence, independence, experience, extension of self, extension of sense, management of self, place, space, power and understanding of place and world. These thematic areas were used to code the data through a close reading to deploy the hermeneutic phenomenological analysis, done with a close reading and coding of the 120,000 words collected through interviews and survey. These thematic areas will be expanded upon below and in Chapter 6.

Meanings of place – Using LBSN to understand places as places

The remainder of this chapter will detail practices and uses of LBSN that were coded and identified as indicative of understanding places as *place*. The concept of place used here is aligned to the Heideggerian notion of Chapter 3: by place, what is being referred to is a meaningful existential locale which is recognised by the person as having a meaning or being meaningful. Place can be understood *phenomenologically* as a lived-in experience that comes from interacting with things in the world.

Previously, this phenomenology has been extended to a *post-phenomenology* by incorporating the body as the embodiment of being-there that interacts with computational interfaces and devices and attunes to the environment suffused with networked information as the site of possibility for interaction with LBSN in understanding place and attunement to the digital world. Code is the agent that makes this possible, acting as the membrane enabling a connection to connected placehood. This view of place understands place itself as a locale where by interacting with things (that is, by treating them with concern and as entities rather than mere extension) the thing orients people towards the world and provides an understanding of place – in this case, the interest is obviously with the interaction with the mobile phone and LBSN. This understanding of things in the world leads to a dwelling in the world, where one understands space as a place that can be thought about, understood and where one can be at "home" in the world (Jacobson, 2006: 1), rather than simply view the world as a disengaged observer. When at "home," humans are dwelling in the world, not homeless in a world that is unfamiliar and bewildering (Jacobson, 2006: 310). It is the practices of using LBSN that result in this kind of understanding that are of interest in the rest of this chapter.

The computational device and LBSN as a thing that reveals place

The orientation of the user to world to understand place is visible through examples of how users report that the device feels like an extension of the user in the world or an extension of their senses. This kind of observation resonates with a McLuhanist interpretation of the relationship between user and medium, but here the focus is obviously on how using the device and LBSN affects the orientation of the user to the world, and how this orientation affects the understanding of place. Acknowledging the McLuhanist influence on this insight and analysis, the macro-category this response was coded in was called *extension of self*, as this comment encompasses the use of LBSN to appreciate and empathise with others in different places.

> There were a couple moments when Foursquare strongly affected my relationship to space and others in it. The first one was when Toronto had its worst earthquake in over a hundred years. It wasn't a big one,

but it was an odd, bewildering experience. I turned on my mobile and noticed that others had been checking into the earthquake (the location was the entire city). I felt much more connected to my fellow city inhabitants somehow through that. I also watched virtually the locations and people of Toronto's G20 protests. Even though these were extensively covered by the media, using Foursquare somehow made it feel more real and nearby opposed to TV that feels distant and foreign even when it is local coverage. (ME05)

This user expresses the experience of being linked to events through a device, extending one's experience beyond passive media reception and feeling part of events that one is spatially separate from, but can feel part of thanks to geo-location data and LBSN. The idea of feeling more connected to other inhabitants during an earthquake by using LBSN signifies an understanding of events in the world (and places) through computation, but also importantly indicates empathy for the other derived from the data provided by the LBSN. This understanding of others and attunement to the local world and the place others are in is facilitated by the computational device, presenting information and ordering a semantically critical representation. The gathering of the symbolic and semantic by the LBSN code and thinking about being (the being of others as empathy) that occurs in this instance is a kind of thinking about other entities and place which is indicative of the appreciation of place that this chapter is interested in.

Some users reported an extension (or replacement) of senses in the world, in how those users understood the world in the way the five senses enable an everyday understanding of the world. In a similar McLuhan-influenced moment, the responses that exemplified this extension of self from the close reading of the ethnography were coded *extension of self* (unoriginally), and are indicative of how the LBSN and computational device take up the cognitive demands of locating oneself in average everyday life (Berry, 2011: 143).

I have a terrible sense of directions and my iPhone has "saved my life" on numerous occasions! (FE13)

Aside from some hyperbole, FE13's sense of direction is explicitly mentioned, criticised, and compared to the certainty provided by the iPhone, which is a lifesaver, in this user's words. Direction is not a sense as understood in the five senses, but can be explained through Kant's notion of space as an *a priori*, pre-experience category of understanding in the world direction is something intuitive and an organising principle upon which experience is shaped (Carnap, 1995: 177–178).

The idea of replacing one's understanding of direction (not a sense, but an understanding of orientation to places in the world) with the iPhone (and therefore LBSN and GPS capabilities realised by the computational processes of the phone) is an important indicator of the event of revealing place and dwelling. The device can, through the provision of data on place encoded in the databanks of the LBSN, replace learned processes of finding one's way in the world and navigating places – in essence: an inability to attune to the world. Without this, a feeling of homelessness occurs without the device; a difficulty in dwelling (or uncanniness) in the world or appreciating place. This kind of practice, replacing an ability one feels is weak with the device's functioning, can again be interpreted as a taking into care; utilising the device as tool and using its functioning to understand place through its gathering of person, information, possibility and finally the understanding obtained through its functioning (dwelling). This is also related to the embodiment and hermeneutic relations to the device outlined in Chapter 4. This notion of the device becoming a replacement for a deficient sense of direction is reiterated:

> Being deprived of this extra sense wouldn't affect my desire or ability but would perhaps make me feel "underpowered" perhaps in a similar way that a heavy cold affects people's sense of taste or smell – they still eat, but don't enjoy it as much. It feels an enhancement of my own capabilities, extending my knowledge about my immediate environs. Even aside from Foursquare, the GPS and map functionality seem to add an extra sense. The GPS abilities of my iPhone do indeed feel like an extra sense; perhaps not one as important as seeing or hearing, but definitely on a par with smell or taste. (ME0712201004)

ME0712201004 identifies the device as an augmentation of their senses, heightening understanding of the world when used and being conspicuous in absence. The identification of the device as an extra sense is also raised; if the senses are considered as the means by which information about the world is collected by the body, then the identification of the device as sense situates the device as a provider of information about the world, which then is interpreted and acted upon as deemed necessary by the user. The device is not a replacement, but an addition to the existing means of collecting information about the world that is the foundation of understanding and prosthesis to attunement. This can also be understood through Ihde's (1990: 73) concept of the embodiment relation where technology is taken as the medium of subjective perceptual experience of the world, transforming the nature of sensation itself for the subject. The pre-existing semantic categorisation and labelling of the information, as provided through the sorting of data into fields in databases and the social gazetteers added by users to the inscriptions of place in the database, means this information about the world is not in a raw form like the information collected by the senses and assimilated by cognitive processes into meaningful information about the world. The device – through linking to this information about the world – is performing the assimilative role of cognitive processes for the user and gives information that is meaningful without cognitive effort. It would be naïve to suggest interpretation is also a given from LBSN and computational devices as the user may choose to act upon information, reject it or completely ignore it but the device is doing some of the work involved in sensation, and therefore understanding the world.

The role of the device in understanding place can be understood as a sophisticated heuristic, with code (that brings information into the understanding of the venue from the databanks of the LBSN) saving cognitive effort by providing the thoughts of others and information that is meaningful for the user without the user having to expend cognitive resources of their own, as would be the case without the device. This technology is radically different from a map (which it could be argued does much the same thing); one is not often inclined to carry maps at all times, whereas the convenient and powerful computational device can act in the manner of carrying maps and augment understanding whenever the user chooses to utilise it. In light of the portable nature of such devices, this could be at any time, in any circumstance that network coverage allows. The revealing of place through device-assisted attunement becomes dependent upon the utilisation of the device in the practice of being-towards understanding place, and hence the status of thing can be ascribed to the device.

Disclosing place and the "self" using LBSN

In Chapter 6, the management of self-image will be considered with regard to how using LBSN to signify being in a place affects, creates and consolidates a kind of "social capital." However, the disclosure of self and location is not just an instrumental act for the accumulation of social capital, but can instead be intimately linked to human situatedness in places through the process of disclosing one's location.

Management of self-image in this revealing of location is a consideration of what it is to be the subject in a data-stream (Berry, 2011: 193) that emerges from the encoding of location and semantic gazetteers, and how one reflects on the use of that data by both other users and other parties that benefit from such data in the understanding of place. This in itself is an awareness of how the use of the device and LBSN situates users in a place, and how this situatedness is disclosed as place to other users. These responses are taken from the macro-category *management*, but differ from those offered in the analysis in the next chapter by emphasising the meaning of their location as location for others and reflecting upon this rather than deriving social capital from the check-in:

> It occurred to me, as I visited a new city and explored new venues there, that a business competitor monitoring my activity stream could make guesses about my business plans and strategy. Not only is there the possibility of user stalking, property burglary, and similar issues, but there are issues surrounding competitive intelligence gathering and "impression management" that are largely not understood. (ME12)

This user is not only aware of the visibility of the data-stream, but also the possibility of interpretation from the stream and what others could infer from the data (see Berry, 2012c). In a discussion of privacy this is relatively interesting, but more importantly it is relevant to a discussion of place, as it emphasises awareness on the part of the user of the security of the data-stream and the role of the audience for that data-stream. Place is revealed as a meaningful locale both for the user and for the audience, that is not passively receiving the stream but could use that data in an active manner to make inferences about the person and their situation. The revealing of place here is two-fold: there is a pre-reflective usage of the device and LBSN to reveal place, and a secondary conspicuousness of the implications of the practice that is pre-reflective in this user's average everydayness. The user is an IT professional, and as such is part of a computational culture in which the use of LBSN is both expected and accepted, but the provision of data through this practice provokes an uncanny reaction that operates in symbiosis with the dwelling or being-at-home with the device and LBSN. The idea of being part of a computational culture that encourages and expects LBSN usage as a towards-which for use of LBSN, is important in assessing the "thinging" of the device in this instance, but the awareness of the possibilities for the data provided is also important to note. The following comment offers another perspective on this:

> I'm aware of it [privacy] but view it as complementary to the rest of my social graph. I don't attempt to modify my behaviour to reflect a different pattern than I have in the "real world." (ME14)

ME14 identifies their activity and data as a "social graph" as opposed to a data-stream, but in the sense of usage, data-stream would be an appropriate synonym and the same point is made. Interestingly, the user admits to not modifying their behaviour for this data-stream, as ME1412 also implied: these are normal, everyday practices for understanding places, not status check-ins for social capital. This chimes with danah boyd's contention (2014) that privacy is important to social media users but that this needs to be mitigated by the need to connect, contribute and share in a social media environment. In a poetic understanding of place and the world, that status is not important, whereas in a technological understanding of the world social, status was of critical importance. The following comment, again, supports this idea of awareness of the impact of the data-stream as important in understanding one's activity, and therefore understanding of how one acts in the world:

> Since I can distribute my check-in to Foursquare only, or to Twitter, or to Facebook, or to all, it increases the way family and friends interact with me as I usually add a note abut the place where I'm checking in giving them an opportunity to reply, or find me, or call me. (MS39)

The key discussion on disclosure of self is summarised nicely in this comment:

> I may as well be blunt about this. Nowadays, people will go and Google you anyway. So you might as well build an image online (rather than letting things people post about you be the only search results they get). I do create online identities under my real name (and at the same time I'm careful when it comes to reputation management). I think that if you have the choice to create/maintain an image, you should take it. I try to sound professional and decent on my social networking accounts in case potential employers find me, but I also like to present myself as a normal person. (FE64)

FE64 shows an awareness of a totalising effect of computation not only on understanding the disclosure of self, but also on how others understand the user. A person must manage their identity (their data-stream) in a world in which other people can utilise computational tools to understand that person and make an impression of that person based on the results those computational tools provide. The disclosure of self and other entities is therefore pro-active, and in an understanding of place as *place* (where place is revealed as place using the device rather than utilisable space) then the letting-come-forth of place as a part of the sharing of location is accepted. Place is not reduced to a status indication for social capital but instead fits with other activities that are computer-mediated to produce data for the data-stream, and disclosure is not a function of selecting high status places to visit but being aware of and reflecting upon the data-stream, who uses that data-stream, and why they use it as part of an awareness of the wider computational culture in which the user dwells. This being-at-home with sharing data and computational practices for understanding place is important in attitude and orientation of a user in a revealing of place as place using LBSN, as it represents both an attunement to device and attunement to the data-infused foam that is the digital world. The creation and sharing of personal location data is an inevitability of using LBSN[4] through the code of the LBSN that orders information on not only the place itself, but also the user and the networks they are part of and contribute data to as participants. These users accept this as part of a trade-off with the LBSN for the revealing of place that can be achieved through the use of the service and explain the consequences of the production of location data about themselves through the wider context of social media and computational culture. As such, this does not inhibit activity when the service is seen as either useful or indispensible to their profession, but instead activity is rationalised and normalised into everyday practices. In addition, the placehood achieved in these examples is a placehood dependent on the social: connecting with others as well as the information banks of the application. Recall that Sloterdijk's "bubbles" (see chapter 4) had at a basic level the dyad of the social. In these examples, the code of LBSN is used to formulate that dyadic (and more) relationship with an integration of the information of the application. In this sense, the social of the LBSN is the formation of that sphere where people are coalesced at a place through the functioning of the device in a Sloterdijkian sphere.

Place revealed poetically

The two comments considered here illustrate how Foursquare can help establish a sense of place for users, with responses appropriately from the macro-category *place*, where the close reading of the replies identified responses that explicitly referenced place in the sense of a meaningful existential locale:

> In specific circumstances the service has made me aware of places around me. The majority of check-ins I make are for places I already know, but there are a few times when I have used Foursquare to find new places. For example, I had to meet some people at a pub in Cheltenham, which I had not been to previously. Using the postcode to find the area on GPS, I then used Foursquare when I had parked the car to navigate to the pub. In York, I used Foursquare to find a pub that was showing a football match I wanted to see by looking for pubs and tips, and then using the map facility. When in places that I don't know unquestionably Foursquare has helped make me more aware of places. (MW11)

MW11 has used the LBSN to find places, and to locate themself relative to those places. Recall the definition of place being used here: a place being somewhere that is meaningful for the user, as it dwells in that place and establishes the meaning of that place based on the relations it has to things in that place, and how it is oriented to those things. Here, the user is employing the LBSN to orient themselves towards the unfamiliar locales, to locate and ground themselves in that locale, transforming the meaningless space of unfamiliarity with the place of familiarity based on the function of code in retrieving information contained in the database of the LBSN, and orienting themselves accordingly. This user of Foursquare uses the LBSN in a similar way:

> Also Indonesia doesn't have proper directories/resources like you'd have in the US or the many parts of Europe, so when I need to find a location, I actually look the venue up on Foursquare (assuming the coordinates are right and an address has been entered). (FE64)

FE64 identifies the same functioning of the LBSN as MW11 (above), but identifies a flaw in the LBSN: that without an entry in the database, orienting oneself in this manner is not possible. This illustrates a limitation in using the LBSN for orienting oneself towards place and a technological understanding of the formatting dictated by entries in the database. If the database were entirely comprehensive then this would not be problematic, but as the user suggests, this is not the case. The possibility of place is therefore a function of the detail of the database used. These contributions provide a helpful illustration of the modern understanding of place: in the first comment, MW11 is engaging with the device to think about where they want to dwell and that thinking is concerned with place. The device acts by gathering the user, the practices of use, the possibilities of where to go, and the thinking that is occurring in this process. In the framework of Chapter 4, this was positioned as the device "thinging," but the possibility of "thinging" is contingent upon the quality of the database of places (and such, code) and the availability of information. Indeed, one could say that the possibility of entering a sphere in Sloterdijk's terms is contingent on the membrane of code. In the second comment, there is an illustration of the device as tool being brought into conspicuousness by being used pre-reflectively as a tool until a lack of functioning creates an opportunity to consider the functioning of the device. If working correctly, the device can – if brought into this kind of care – create a local existential locale for thinking about place, but this is contingent on the availability of the database and connectivity to that database. If realised, the possibility of disclosing place and dwelling in that place is possible. The use of devices to reveal location to others while fully aware of this disclosure and in a way that reveals the place as meaningful is what I argue is an alternative to the technological or modern revealing of space.

From the ethnography, key responses emphasise the necessity of the device for revealing place and the practices of revealing place as a meaningful existential locale. These practices of use are critical when one considers how the computational device is brought into care to allow it as a thing to reveal the placehood of the place (rather than setting forth place as a challenge to the user to be overcome and harnessed as resource). The following examples of such usage are taken from the macro-analysis category *behaviour*, where behaviour explicitly refers to examples of the use of LBSN in understanding place in the average everyday context of users' lives that emerged from the close reading of responses:

> I will occasionally pick an area of town that is a total wreck and its information on Google Maps is lacking. I'll keep my laptop in my car and walk around the area marking areas and taking photos to correct the 4sq database. (ME15)

In actively engaging in finding areas that are poorly served by existing LBS and LBSN services, this user is displaying practices consistent with the appreciation of place. The user is searching to improve the service, and carries (embodies) the necessary equipment to make corrections and additions to the database of places that constitute the LBSN. This kind of behaviour is atypical; the user is a "level 3 Superuser" on Foursquare and obviously one that takes that responsibility (of maintaining the quality and integrity of the data on the LBSN accurate) seriously. The user is oriented towards using his devices in finding and ascribing place to spaces in the world. This is a user that is carrying about computational equipment for the sake of the LBSN and database, and his behaviour is indicative of a for-the-sake-of-which that is oriented to using LBSN to understand place. If the database is not up-to-date and of quality, then the need to understand place through computational means is frustrated and action to correct this is taken using the tools that one would use to understand place meaningfully. The practice being described is a using of the device to actively understand place, and as such should be understood as a taking of the device into care for the towards-which of understanding place, but that this understanding is in itself mediated by the LBSN. This user illustrates a dependence upon LBSN and an immersion in a computational environment in which LBSN plays an important role and is a legitimate way of locating oneself and understanding place. Another user that describes usage in similar terms:

> When first engaged in the enthusiasm of trying out [Foursquare] I found myself walking around, iPhone in hand, so that I could check in to places more quickly. (ME12)

The user is making conscious acknowledgement of charting their own behaviour with the LBSN and that service being an active part of their everyday behaviour. The device as a computational "coded object" (Berry, 2012b) is directing and orienting action in this instance. The user is aware of the physical characteristics of the "coded object" as a part of their action, and thinking about the computational device and the LBSN in the course of their daily movements in the world. It is illustrative of the need to use the computational device in the world, to engage with it and to use the device as an active part of the everyday being-in-the-world (care). The following response emphasises the use of the device as part of everyday behaviour, and in doing so is linking the everyday practices of locating oneself and others explicitly with using LBSN to reveal place as an existential locale that is meaningful socially, rather than as co-ordinates.

> I think the device is becoming a tool for navigating with these services. If I did not have the device then it would affect the people side of

things, for me its [sic] good to know where other people are – there is a term, ambient awareness – and its [sic] like that; you can come out of the cinema, and if you're looking for somewhere to drink and you're on your own you just check where people are and then you go and join them. That happens quite a lot. People will also talk about events that other people have been to, because they've seen where they are on the phone, so there is a dynamic social thing going on rather than a venue thing. The social thing is the big one for me, because that is the primary benefit. It could come across in the wrong kind of way as stalking but it's a tighter circle on foursquare than on Facebook. If I walk past certain places that I know people drink in, I'll check to see if they are in there and if they are there I'll pop-in and say hi, so it works well from that perspective I think. (MP20)

The behaviour described by this user – again, a level 3 Superuser – is interesting from the social perspective that the user is so keen to emphasise. In using the LBSN to create impromptu social interactions with friends, then there is a computationally dependent behaviour exhibited and enacted that can be argued to be a departure from previous social behaviour. While using mobile phones as social facilitators is not new, it is the use of the LBSN that is indicative of a modern revealing of place. Consider some common practices of social facilitation using the mobile phone: one might send an SMS message, or indeed phone friends, ask them where they are and meet at the place they are at that time. What this user shows is that is that someone that uses the LBSN frequently can know where people are relative to them and also predict the movements of people for social interactions. This behaviour brings the LBSN, device, place and user together as elements, and shows a gathering of a kind. When the thing "things" here, mortals, skies, earth and divinities are brought together. The mortals are clearly people; the sky the possibilities of meeting; the earth the practices of using LBSN to create the meeting; the divinity the bringing together of these elements in the meeting and the dwelling of the social space. If LBSN is a computational thing that things, then it is in this kind of behaviour, action and being that the "thinging" would be active, creating an "existential locale" which is contingent upon the LBSN and the device for its existence. It is the manner of this meeting, the towards-which of the user (towards-others or Dasein-with others) and the patterns of behaviour and using of the device that is of interest. The user also acknowledges the change in practices and the importance of the device and LBSN and offers some guidance as to how the computational thing "thinging" can be a possibility. The discourse analysis revealed a series of replies that emphasised the use of Foursquare to locate others:

> It helps me stalk friends – I mean that in a good way. (MS33)

> Now I use it to stalk and be stalked – I find it interesting to have the impromptu meet-ups it enables. (MS44)

Tracking others becomes an acknowledged behaviour that is even desirable. Again, the possibility of meeting people by using the LBSN is praised as a positive behavioural possibility of using the device. There is little reflection upon privacy and the danger of revealing location in these responses, just that sharing location can be beneficial socially and that this is "good" (although this appears to be changing in some instances). The sharing of location is seen as something that can be positive socially rather then just used as data to be exploited, and that proximity can be a function of shared concerns, social interests and interactions that transcend physical proximity when facilitated by computational processes (see Coyne, 1995: 10; Greenfield, 2006: 126). This comment emphasises that point:

> It's especially useful for that at large conferences and I've used it to enable me to meet up with people that I wanted/needed to connect with. (MS33)

MS33 identifies social gatherings that are facilitated by the LBSN, and again is indicative of bringing the LBSN into care as a tool to locate and understand place. This is a computational practice of understanding places and social interaction, and points towards a wider use of the LBSN amongst this user group (academics attending conferences) for social activity. If one person is using the LBSN to obtain information on others, then it follows that others are checking-in at places and that person is accessing their data to ascertain their whereabouts. The event of revealing place here is achieved through the practices not only of the user, but also of other users. This implies that the "thinging" of the thing is contingent on the use of LBSN by others and this social dimension is something important when considering the practices involved in the revealing of place by the device and LBSN. This was a feature of a number of replies from users:

> I occasionally have twitter friends turn up at the pub, and the fact they know some of my movements does obviously change interactions

later. It also means the first couple of minutes after arriving at any particular venue are spent rummaging around and checking in. (MS44)

Once or twice, I've called/SMS'ed friends who were nearby that I would have normally missed. (MS34)

MS44 and MS34 comment on their practices of use of the LBSN as linked to social interaction, and the computational device and LBSN becomes a part of their everyday social practices. The device is an enabler and as such is embodied and used pre-reflectively in these circumstances. These practices engage the users with places and reveal space as potential or actual social space for interaction and activity: an acute attunement to the possibilities of place. Responses that could be interpreted as illustrating a dependence on the device can be interpreted as an integration of the device into the everyday practices of understanding place that is harmed when the device is unavailable or broken. The use of the device and LBSN as an indispensible part of finding routes and ways to places was emphasised as a part of everyday behaviour in a number of responses:

Being able to just get my location and directions to something has become an integral part of our lives. Also, it's saved our bacon a couple of times when we're trying to get somewhere and gotten lost or off-track. (ME17)

ME17 stresses the integral nature of the GPS and LBSN elements of their computational device in their everyday life. The qualification of that importance through the concrete scenario that the service has saved them when getting lost is also important. In many cases, one will use the GPS enabled device to plot a route. The user has used the device when "place" is lost, to orient themselves in their location by calling on the "code object" and for it to place the user in relation to other places and their distance. This kind of practice is bringing the device into care as a tool, and the device becomes conspicuous in (potential or perceived) absence. The use of the device is accepted as everyday practice, and it "things" in the process of locating oneself and understanding place. The following comment illustrates using LBSN as a way of orienting oneself to the world as a more integral part of everyday life:

While some people would see it as a sad thing, I have a hard time venturing out into the urban world without some kind of technological enhancement to it. I like seeing things coming. I like seeing a marker for something new that's a couple blocks away, and going to see what it is. It's that whole "See shiny thing, poke at shiny thing" instinct that many creatures of the world have. I just have a phone to show me the shiny things, and without this phone, the world would be, to finish the analogy, quite dull. This dependence has also made me realize that I'm likely not alone. There's probably some other person out there who likes to use their phone all the time. (ME15)

The dependence on the device and LBSN here is very specific. ME15 admits to having difficulty functioning without the device and even envisaging functioning without the device and the LBSN as it gives the user the ability to "see" what is approaching. This pre-emptive navigation – an understanding of where the user is going before they get there – is again something that could be done with paper maps, but the ideas expressed are both that the phone provides information in an useful and compelling way and that the social, sharing facility marks the device and LBSN as different to paper maps.

The way the device and LBSN combine to present information (through accessing the database and providing a data stream on places in the locale) is again something that can be considered a gathering in this instance. The user thinks about the world when the possibilities of action (skies) are shown, the practices of use for location (earth) are enacted, the user (mortal) is present and there is a feeling of using the device that is positively affirmed by the user (divinity). The kind of thinking that occurs here is interesting when reflecting on the possibility of the device being a "thing." In this case, the user's experience of the world (indeed, the possibility of moving in the world) is attributed to the functioning of the device, and how this device operates in allowing the user affordances that comforts them in how they move through the angst-provoking world (Young, 2000: 189). Some users commented on how not having the device would inconvenience their everyday life as the behaviours of finding place would be disrupted:

Yes – accidentally leaving them [previous phones] at home was mildly inconvenient, whereas if I left this phone at home I would go back for it (even if it made me late). (ME04)

Much more so my iPhone has become an indispensible navigational device, not just when using Foursquare but also Layar, skobbler and other applications. The device is not just a phone, and to be honest the functionality as a phone is probably the least important function of the phone to me – it's the connection to other services which I have come to use much more since getting the device. The device is unquestionably more integral to my life than previous mobile devices, and foursquare and GPS is important in that. Whether the GPS facility is more important than twitter or email or net access I don't know – I think all these things have made the device important. (MW11)

ME04 shows how computational functionality has for this user made the device indispensible, even to the extent of changing plans rather than being without the device. MW11 further argues that as the device is no longer just a phone but has computational functionality that makes the device indispensible, with LBSN and LBS being a part of this integral role in the everyday life of the user. Place is understood through the practices of location and navigation using the applications available on the device, and without this the user has a feeling of "homelessness." In considering dwelling with LBSN, this uncanny feeling of being lost without the device implies that the device is needed to achieve a "dwelling," and the comportment towards space of the user is a function of their use of the device and LBSN.

Users that have brought the device and LBSN into their average everydayness as a means to understand place (the towards-which of understanding place) and situate the LBSN in their everyday practices as part of a set of computational practices in everyday life have a towards-which that allows for the revealing of place through the device. The event is dependent upon the initial towards-which of Dasein and the practices of use of the LBSN and functioning of code. This account of *placehood* accentuates the "thinging" of the thing and how industrial and modernist notions of place are giving way to place-mediated technology. Before considering the practices and orientations towards the world that are indicative of this shifting understanding of place, there is the issue of identifying what practices and orientations towards devices contribute to a technological (or modernist, industrial) revealing of place using computational devices and LBSN. Chapter 6, therefore, will assess what orientations and usage prevent bringing the device into care as part of the gathering of elements by the thing, and what such a technological revealing of place is in the practice of using LBSN.

"Self as blue dot"

Responses in the ethnography that explicitly discussed how place was revealed and understood by using the LBSN were coded in the macro-category *world*. This category arose in the close reading of the ethnography from responses that emphasised the role of the LBSN as part of a wider computational culture in which the user lives in (*world*), or an indication that the device and LBSN form part of the average, everyday life of the user and have been integrated into that average everydayness as a normative art of being (*worldhood*). The reasons for using Foursquare itself can be revealing in that they can offer indications of what kind of orientations with regards to the device are pre-cursors of the understanding of place:

> I had to try out the new thing I heard about at SXSW 2009 and it seemed like a fun thing to do which I could use the location features of my iPhone. (FS30)

> I stumbled across it via someone on Twitter, from memory, when I noticed that someone I was following on Twitter was notifying everyone of where they were at any given time. (FS32)

> Saw people "checking in" on Facebook and thought that's cool. (FS38)

> I thought it would be useful socially. Originally, I saw other friends "checking-in" places and I thought it would be helpful to know if my friends were in my neighbourhood. (FS52)

> I always like to try out new Web 2.0/social network services as soon as I hear about them. (MS46)

The collection of comments here illustrate that Foursquare exists as part of a wider cultural frame of computationally-mediated communications tools such as Facebook or Twitter which users are familiar with, at home with and attuned to in their everyday lives. This indicates of course that these users were already engaged with Twitter and Facebook, and that those services and the information provided through status updates, tweets and posts to news feeds has an influence on those users. LBSN is part of a computational culture where services are discussed and gain approval, and users add the service due to a wider cultural influence. These users were engaged with other digital services, and regarded them as part of their everyday routines and behaviours before using LBSN. This immersion in digital technology is therefore an aspect in how a worlding that allows for the poetic revealing of place using LBSN occurs. Before explaining a modern understanding of place through the use of the device, the route to any such disclosure is already characterised by the wider cultural frame in which users exist and which informs their decisions; what Berry (2011, 2012b) calls *computationality*. In Chapter 4, Sloterdijk's concept of the globalised foam (that is characteristic of networked places) would offer an explanation for this computational frame of reference, as the continual connectivity, and making and breaking of connections using this connectivity is a constitutive feature of foam.

The revealing of place is indicative of an orientation to the world that brings the computational device into average everyday circumspection and use, rather than just being influenced by information mediated computationally but ultimately derived from friends, acquaintances or family. The following comment illustrates what is meant by such a being-towards or comportment:

> I mark it anywhere I go, if I remember to do it. It's sometimes a conversation starter with friends on Twitter and Facebook. It makes me feel like I'm not living quite so invisibly. (FS37)

FS37 explains their behaviour in the context of providing information for socialising and the idea of a visibility for their lives. Both these justifications for using the LBSN relate to the data-stream that their activity produces, and therefore their activity (of using the LBSN) is with full awareness of the creation and sharing of information across social networks. The comment on the visibility of their life is a reference to the visibility of the information they provide via the LBSN through the encoding of location and semantic gazetteers as a data-stream to other users (and themselves), and as part of a worlding through using the device that connects their actions to digital sharing practices and being visible through computational means, which is afforded by the computational functioning of the device (through its use of code). The following comment acknowledges a similar approach to usage:

> Because I post to Facebook with Foursquare, it lets my distant family see a little of our normal activities, especially with my younger daughter's soccer and Girl Scout events. (FS37)

FS37's contributions to their personal data-stream contribute to the knowledge of a specific audience, which is their distant family. The comment emphasises how the mediation of location through the device and LBSN becomes part of the average everydayness of the user, and the media becomes a form of what Merrin (2014) calls me-dia, in that it facilitates a form of horizontal, peer-to-peer communication with the person and their immediate and chosen social groups and friends. The emergence of this me-dia can be seen as a challenge to the impersonality of public spaces that Sennett (2003) argues has become a feature of modernity, albeit in a hyper-localised and particular form in making place and activity visible to others in a meaningful manner. Foursquare allows others to see a part of the user's normal activities and this acknowledges an integration of this computationally medi-ated communication into everyday life. The visibility of activity in the data-stream has become, for this user, an important aspect of everyday life. Borrowing from Bassett (2012: 113–114), even the game aspect of the use of LBSN can be seen as contributing to the narrative of life history as the gaming "bleeds" into real, everyday life as a relationship between the symbolic aspect of the LBSN and the "real" of discussing, sharing and charting experiences and everyday life. The computational being-towards everyday activity is a key aspect of this understanding of place, in that understanding the importance of the visibility of oneself and one's activity through computational means is a critical part of knowing how one must act in a world with computational devices. In practice, the user can perceive such an understanding of place and the world beneficially:

> Foursquare has made keeping up with my best friend, who moved back to the United States in February of this year, easier as I can see what she's up to and where she is. (FS32)

FS32 is again using the data-stream to understand place (in this case to make meaningful their distant friend's activities with regards to place), which adds a level of significance to the information provided. The understanding is dependent upon the LBSN and data-stream surfacing the possibility of place for the user and is possible because of the computational functionality of the device, running the code of the LBSN and connecting to servers. The user can understand the aver-age everydayness of the other using the LBSN and data-stream, and the global space that separates the two users is reduced to a local relation-ship as the position of the other is transformed by the mediation of place through the LBSN. This is enabled by the orientation of the user, in that there is a desire to understand the location and situatedness of the other person as a meaningful location, rather than superfluous information – as place, rather than space. The information produced, stored and provided allows for an understanding of place that was not possible previously, and is not necessarily technological in disclosure, as this comment acknowledges:

> It has made me more aware of what friends are doing and where they are, but it hasn't been a world-changing thing. Not as much as, say, having the Internet in general (and in particular Google and Wikipedia) at my fingertips 24x7 no matter where I am (as long as I get coverage *grin*). (ME17)

The recognition of the continual connectivity of the device and the software that relies upon this connectivity as a service to understand place is an extension of the previous comments. What is also useful in ME17's comment is in parenthesis; this understanding is again dependent upon information, but that information stream is again contingent upon connectivity. That connectivity is now a vital part of everyday life is obvious but in a situation where one is using a device to understand the places in which one is located then connectivity becomes critically important. This comment further illustrates the importance of sharing and social networking in this worldview:

> Admittedly, I'm one of those people who probably over-shares thinking someone cares about it. Like I said before, I use most social media for my own sake. I know I'm just some guy, and I'm probably quite dull, but I like to keep a memory of my life backed up somewhere. Plus, you never know who might get curious. Perhaps I'm relying on my dull nature to prevent someone malicious from stalking me? (ME15)

ME15's self-reflection draws the discussion of the disclosing through data-streams to a close, as it provides an opportunity to discuss the data-stream as a reflective device to think about being, which would indicate that the device and LBSN (and any other service that contributes to or presents one's data-stream) have a role in thinking about being. The importance of this will be acknowledged in Chapter 5: in Heidegger's notion of dwelling, when one dwells one has cleared room for thinking about being (2008: 335), facilitated by things that gather the four-fold elements together for a dwelling to occur (Heidegger, 2008: 337). Stiegler's (1998: 174) concept of *epiphylogenesis* is also useful in considering this reflection. Culture becomes possible itself through the inorganic organisation of memory, and the data-stream is a way of organising in this manner. In doing this, the data-stream makes culture possible (and therefore the possibility of reflection upon said culture is possible). By exteriorising oneself technologically (Stiegler, 1998: 141), there is the possibility of knowing being by being able to project oneself from the past into future action. This point can be developed further in light of Chun's (2011: 137) argument that software is always embodied, and in being embodied it grounds memory; doing this creates an "enduring ephemeral" that has the promise of lasting forever. In this case, that forever is temporally bound as the future. Parikka (2012: 90) also contributes to this line of thought, arguing that digital memory forces a re-thinking of memory, perception, collection and organisation. Software-based cultural memories reveal the digital humanities to be an area of study of the calculations and algorithms which process information on non-discursive platforms. As such, a phenomenology of new media (which LBSN would be an important part of) is grounded in an understanding and awareness of calculations based on algorithm, process and address (in a database) taking the place of spaces. The mechanisms and operations of software and code are therefore critical in both the possibility and actuality of this externalisation of memory, projection of activity, and externalisation of the self through digital means.

It would be easy to suggest that in the presence of an ever-updated, fast moving data-stream that we are only going to be in a state of harassed unrest (Heidegger, 2008: 328), continually bombarded with data with no time or inclination to think about that data in a meaningful way. However, consider the forms of thinking that have been identified in this section: a concern for the movement of other people who are meaningful for the user; acknowledgement of one's own presence as a data-stream or provider of data to a stream; and some recognition that without being an active stream the user is absent from the thoughts of others – not visible[5] – and therefore not available for others to reflect upon. Thus, the device and LBSN (or other service) should be understood here as a thing – a computational thing that is data- or information-driven, and as such does not provide information only as resource (although this as an element of the view cannot be dismissed entirely) but also as something that can be reflected upon to bring others and oneself into circumspection (see Berry, 2011).

In considering worldhood and how experience of the world is altered with the presence of the device and the LBSN, a number of comments point to role of the device as vital in everyday life, without being dependent in a technological sense:

> If once in the past I had to get a map or driving directions, nowadays I ask for the address and get places with the GPS, which is easier for

both sides – I don't have to remember everything and the other side just gives an address, or says "this coffee place" and I can get the address from the internet. Before the iPhone I had dumb phones, no GPS or Internet in that level, so I was more limited. (ME09)

ME09 emphasises the perceived ease of everyday life with the LBSN and the a-GPS enabled device, in that less effort is required on their part and some anguish is avoided in finding places. What is of interest here is the brief clause "I don't have to remember everything;" the device is positioned as an addition to the cognitive capabilities of the user and as something that can be utilised to reduce the cognitive effort that the user expends in navigating the world. This questions how the user views their position in the world with the device. What needs to be considered is: if the user considers the device to be doing some of the cognitive work of being a human in the world, how does the user consider the device in light of this? The following comment is also useful in this context:

When I drive down the road with my phone docked, I see that little blue and white dot on the screen. I realize that's me, and I see all the cars around me, and realize they have dots too. I'm just another face in the world. If you'll pardon the slightly obscure reference, it makes me feel like Haruhi Suzumiya when she went to a baseball game in the city as a little girl, and saw all those people in the stands, and realized her special life wasn't so special anymore. Unlike her, I lack the drive to go find strangeness in the world on my own. I suppose programs that are aware of where I am has given me a bit of a drive to explore this big world. I have a guide that I can fall back on, and that lets me go out and explore a bit more. I mean, what's that strange landmark on 4sq called Stabber's Alley? Just how dark and foreboding is it? Better go see during the day. (ME15)

ME15 identifies with the device, and the denotation of the device on the digital map (the "blue dot") as *themselves*, so the distinction between user and device withdraws in use as location is established, disclosed and understood as a co-construction between device, space and user. The user extrapolates their own experience and position in the world relative to the device to others by identifying other people as dots, in line with the withdrawal of the distinction between device and user in their own experience.

The device, which is doing the work of locating oneself in the world in this instance, is not considered separately as an entity. While this view of the device can lend itself to a post-humanist analysis of the relationship between user and device, this is a phenomenological study and there is not the space to consider this here. The experience of the device as one with the user – withdrawn when used as a tool – is one of absence, but as the device is continually updating, representing the world as one moves through the world physically, it is becoming present, demanding attention and thinking. The device is something that links with other things (servers, databases, other devices) beyond the conscious experience and is continually feeding back to the user. Ihde (1990: 86) explains this as the alterity relation between technology and human where the technology acts as an immediate referent to something beyond that device. While the focus of the user is on the device and interface, the user's experience is not with the device itself but the world that it is referring to and the landscape suggested by the gazetteers. In this case, the device withdraws (while still performing the work it is tasked with in revealing the world) to become part of the world.[6] This view is reinforced by this comment:

> think my view of the world has changed by using these services – or at least how I view the world. When visiting new places I used to stick to small areas, which I could achieve familiarity with quite easily, whereas now using location-based services means that I can use the device with confidence to locate myself and familiarize myself with the place. I am aware that there is a contradiction in that, in that I am only familiarizing myself with the representation of the place from the service, and so there is a tension between familiarity with place and service – and in considering how I see the world, I suppose I am seeing it more through the device than through exploring it physically. (MW11)

MW11 is aware that they are familiarising themselves with the device, interface and service, and that the result of this is a familiarity with place that is dependent upon the device and software. The nature of the tool – what it does – as a navigational tool, as something to guide the user through the world, is clear. As a tool, it is withdrawn from conscious appreciation when used, that is being used to navigate, and it is reasonable to suggest that in the case of the user this is the case, but the user is aware of how the device is a transformational influence through its representation of the world. The device is active even while used as a tool, and it is this that is critical in how the computational device and LBSN provides an understanding of place. The real time information is given unobtrusively, so not removing the device from being ready to use (continuing its presence as a co-constructing element in the understanding and revealing of place), keeping it always operational and ready to disrupt: never fully withdrawn from conscious awareness. This tension informs the worldview which is based on computation and shapes this understanding of world, and is a major theme of analysis in Chapter 6.

A final comment shows how continual information given in real-time by the device affects understanding of the world, and changes orientation to the world in a practical way for place and location:

> Suddenly the ability to ask for directions is lost! In the past I'd often end up wandering around new places relatively aimlessly but it was just as good as going somewhere specific because that kind of wandering can lead to making new discoveries. If you are headed in a very specific direction with a very clear aim, you might risk missing things along the way, which is a shame. (FE07)

There are two important issues in this comment. With the device (assuming connectivity is a given) the existential possibility of being lost is reduced, and if the technological conditions are optimal then being lost could be something that is technologically not possible. The most interesting issue raised is the idea that something important in itself is lost if one cannot get lost. The chance discovery, the valuable new place found, the orienting oneself in the unfamiliar place that leads to a new familiarity, and the creation of an existential locale through orienting oneself to the objects and entities in the new locale. One could argue that Foursquare is *for* the chance discovery or valuable new place, but the user identifies that this is not the same kind of discovery as an unaided one. The directing of the user towards places in the database means that chance is removed from the experience, according to the user. The revealing of place is dependent on the device, as being lost or "placeless" is not a possibility if one has taken the device into care as a part of the average everydayness of navigating the world. This is only possible though in the computationally-infused environment that these users exist in. If this is done, then place as a familiar existential locale is always possible through the use of the device as a co-constructor of the sense of place in the world.

Summary

From this ethnography and critical discourse reading of the user responses we can see that there are practices that are typical of the device of anticipating and locating others within a community of LBSN users. Users are actively using their devices to locate themselves in a novel space, and to understand that space. Using the device in this manner, as an everyday part of one's life for understanding place, is the focal practice of attunement or orientation that allows for the understanding of place to come forth through the device's functioning. This is the kind of orientation to the device that results in the revealing of place. This orientation relies on the LBSN as an information creating and distributing system through the functioning of the code of the application. This occurs in a manner that allows the user to be contemplative, without inhibiting the use of the service that has become central to the everyday practices of the user. Far from being an inevitable use of LBSN, the revealing of place using LBSN is dependent upon the user using the device in particular ways (or with particular practices of use) as part of their average everyday behaviours and is contingent upon the extent to which computation is a part of their everyday life. The next chapter will consider practices of use that reveal quite different, less "deep" understandings of place.

6
The Social Capital of Locative Social Media

The accumulation of capital through being somewhere could seem, at first, an odd concept. Humans are always "somewhere" and, as such, what is being proposed here is that this necessary and unavoidable facet of being human may be a commodity to be traded. Of course, from one perspective a link between commoditisation and location is obvious; the use of programmes and applications that accumulate data on where you are, what you are doing, who you do this activity with, how often you do this, and what times of the day you do this at sounds like gold to advertisers, and a political economy approach to the use of location-based social networking would concentrate on this aspect of the commoditisation of space. This chapter takes a different approach; the focus here is not on how value as a financial commodity is extracted or created for places in their encoding in databases of places that are used by LBSN, but instead on the practices of users that frame places as a particular kind of commodity. That commodity is social capital, the result of the use of LBSN to create an impression on other users, connections, friends or acquaintances that is positive or that is perceived positively by others. This is not revealing place as *place*; this is revealing place as resource.

The term social capital is not new by any means, but in the context of this study there is a very specific meaning to the term that requires definition before proceeding into analysis. Pierre Bourdieu (1985: 246) defined social capital as "the aggregate of the actual or potential resources which are linked to possession of a durable network of more or less institutionalized relationships of mutual acquaintance and recognition." This is a useful definition to work with here, as the idea of the network obviously links to the structural element of LBSN as a social network where information is not just shared with the application itself, but also with the other people that we are connected to in our social networks. The potential resource in the case of Foursquare users is their location, and following Bourdieu's definition the location of the person that is shared can be a part of the social capital that a person enjoys as part of their social networking activities (both using internet-based social networks and non-electronically mediated social networks). A location that has a high status, such as a popular landmark, high-profile club or nightspot, or place associated with a famous event, could be an example of a place that can leverage an element of social capital in this context. The location need not be well-known, however; a comic book aficionado could, through the sharing of location as a comic book shop, leverage social capital with their connections, with a less well-known location that has social capital in a community of shared interests.

In the mid-1990s, Robert Putnam (1995) argued that social capital was a declining feature of public life, and that this had implications for the building of and maintenance of committees and democracy in western societies. This analysis, of course, pre-dates the emergence of computer-mediated social networking such as Friendster from 2002, and its successors MySpace, Facebook and Twitter (amongst many others). LBSN should be situated as a continuation of such services and applications, adding the element of location-sharing to the practices of profile-building, status-sharing and connection-making that define these services as social networking sites. Online social capital or socio-technical capital can be differentiated from offline social capital due to the unique affordances online tools provide for communicating with a wide range of people instantly (Ellison et al., 2011: 127). Resnick (2001) suggests the construct of sociotechnical capital can be considered as a subset of social capital in order to highlight the ways in which social and technical components "jointly influence the ability of people to act together" (p. 249, in Ellison et al., 2011: 129). It is also useful to note that social capital that is accrued in social networking sites is now quantified; the application Klout aggregates the reach and popularity of one's contributions to social networking platforms and produces a score from 1–100 based on the "influence" that a person has as a social networking site user (Foursquare is a service that can be used in the calculation of a Klout score).

The common differentiation used in theory between bridging and bonding social capital creates a major problem when conceptualising social capital in the use of LBSN. Putnam discusses the two types in his seminal work *Bowling Alone*, and it is worthwhile defining what is meant by the terms and contextualise the problematisation of social capital when considering LBSN here. *Bridging* social capital is credited to Avis Vidal, and refers to the social capital accrued between socially heterogeneous groups. *Bonding* social capital refers to social capital accrued between homogenous social groups, and is attributed to Ross Gittell. In terms applicable to the study in case here, we are discussing the social capital shared between strong social ties (bonding or homogenous) and between weak social ties (bridging or heterogeneous). In the previous chapter, where the use of LBSN was discussed with reference to deep understandings of place as a meaningful locale, the kind of social capital discussed could be understood as bonding, where information is shared with and derived from trusted or known individuals within the network – although this conceptualisation is less than ideal when we consider that some information on place would be obtained from other users that we might know nothing about. Nevertheless, there is a trust in the information provided to understand place, and a sharing of location with existing social ties across social networks. It would be wrong to suggest that all sharing of location is directed towards this kind of social capital though; through a basic macro-reading of the ethnographic material of this study, it is clear that some uses of LBSN fall far away from what would be conceived of as a means of accruing bonding social capital.

Before explaining that point further, it is worth unpacking the complexities involved with social capital and LBSN. The literature on social capital relevant to this investigation covers two distinct forms of media – mobile phones and social networking. LBSNs obviously run on mobile phones, but also are social networks in their own right and importantly can be cross-posted into other social networks (in order to be used for social capital across other networks). This initially may not seem a problem, but the literature on social capital in social networking and mobile phones is not exactly complimentary. Wilken's (2011) comprehensive review of literature on social capital and mobile phones (in Ling and Campbell, 2011: 127–150) identifies that most research has provided ample evidence that mobile phone communications in general work to strengthen strong ties or bonding forms of social capital (2011: 150), but that in certain situations there is evidence that mobile technology can be used to establish and strengthen weak ties or bridging forms of social capital. This latter research taps into examples of social networking on mobile phones, as mobiles become the technology that is increasingly used to access social networks (especially in developing economies).

The extensive literature on social networking and social capital is also complex; Ellison, Steinfield and Lampe (2011) report that information-seeking behaviours on Facebook (an example could be looking for information on location) contribute to perceptions of social capital, but behaviours that focus on close friends do not contribute to bridging capital. Vitak and Ellison (2013) found that Facebook can facilitate both bridging and bonding social capital, and therefore it is the particular practices of use that require close inspection – which the previous chapter and this chapter are obviously paying close attention to with regard to LBSN use. The distinction of bonding social capital (sharing with friends) and bridging social capital (sharing with weak ties) as a salient feature of social networking (in particular Facebook) is confirmed by Burke, Marlow and Lento (2010), Burke, Kraut and Marlow (2011) and Yang, Kurnia and Smith (2011) amongst many others. The scene is much more complex than simply mobile communication = bonding, social networking = bridging.

In the specific case of LBSN though, there is less literature from which to draw firm conclusions. Humphries' (2008) study of Dodgeball (an important precursor of Foursquare, which was discussed in Chapter 2) is empirically one of the few guidance points for this study. Humphries reports that there was considerable use of Dodgeball in the finding out about places and sharing information on location, with strong social ties, that is commensurate with bonding social capital. However, Humphries also reported (pp. 349–350) that many users of the older LSBN would share information to show off, and even those that used the LBSN in a manner commensurate with bonding social capital would, on occasion, use the LBSN to check into a place for the "show-off" value of that place. In essence, this would be an overt practice for the accrual of bridging social capital that can, at the same time, still be used in the accrual of bonding social capital. It is this kind of behaviour and practice of using LBSN that this chapter is interested in, and is termed "screenic" because the place itself (and understanding the place) is not as important as the presence of a user's location being on the "screen" – the newsfeed of their links on social networks.

Obviously then, the purpose of the use of LBSN becomes important when considering the quantification of such interactions as a measure of social capital; the measurement presupposes that users can create or improve a social impression that is in itself instrumental in achieving a goal of creating and maintaining a favourable impression with other people. Putnam's concern was that modern society (that is, society in the 1990s) had atomised human subjectivity and existence in the world, which did not allow for the public expression of attitudes, opinions and personal preferences and had a debilitating effect on public discourse.

While an argument that proposes that social networking sites have solved these problems is fraught with problems, the idea that the structural features of such systems that allow for information to be shared rapidly amongst other people connected to the same network and with a personal connection to the person does allow for the presupposition that social capital can now be obtained through information that is submitted to, shared with and consumed by other users of social networks.

Bridging social capital is, in this context, potentially valuable locational information that will improve the perception of the person sharing that information amongst their connections in a social network. This again emphasises the importance of the sharing of information in an economic context; however, the focus of this chapter is to understand the practices and uses of LBSN that create the possibilities of sharing location as social capital, with a view to analysing the phenomenological importance of this orientation to place. In short, this chapter will explore the manifestations of the need to accrue social capital in Foursquare users through the practices of use and attitudes towards places that were expressed in their responses in the ethnographic study.

Accordingly, this chapter offers a detailed account of responses from Foursquare users that emphasised the sharing of location as a way to elicit positive responses of impressions from other connections in their social networks. It is worthwhile foregrounding just why this should be of concern, and its importance in the context of the phenomenological investigation that is being undertaken in this work. The previous chapter discussed uses of Foursquare where users reported having an increased or improved understanding of place from their engagement with their mobile devices and LBSN application. This chapter discusses a quite different aspect of the use of LBSN: the reduction of place to information to be shared. Rather than understanding place as a meaningful existential locale, the uses of LBSN discussed in this chapter are indicative of a negation of the meaning and features of the location and a focus on how the meaning of the location can be understood as a feature of shared information on social networks rather than a place that the user wants to understand. Whereas previously Foursquare was seen as a tool that could help understand places, in this chapter it creates practices of use that reduce place down to a form of bridging social capital.

To reiterate, the use of the device in this chapter is "screenic," in that the device and LBSN is used in a manner that provides a representation of physical space that lacks the depth (and hence provides "flat" maps of co-ordinates and space for exploitation) of the semantic, relational totality of place that is revealed in a poetic revealing of place. The practices of use, orientations of users and attunements to physical space in this chapter are therefore seen in the context of mapping in the development of the OS and other mapping systems (see Chapter 2) as a technological, modern representation of space and the revealing of space through the screen.

"Technological" use of Foursquare

Casting back to Chapter 2, technological or "modern" uses of mapping technology were described as a reductive representational form where territory is represented in terms of military, economic or political significance. The "technological" use of LBSN is proposed here as the use of the LBSN as a means to signify social importance and leverage social capital. For example, when using Foursquare, users will check-in to "mark territory" or chart their movements for themselves or others. This can be considered as a technological revealing of place in that it involves an appreciation of the LBSN and device as an extension of the behaviour of the user in everyday life, but there is not an appreciation of a change in understanding of place in these operations. An analysis of why users chose to use the LBSN brought some understanding of what patterns of use of LBSN characterise a technological world-revealing of place. These responses are descriptive of choices of how the user uses LBSN and how these actions are part of their everyday lives.

> I wanted to see what Foursquare had to offer and why it was gaining such momentum. Still not sure what they are offering, but now it's become more of a daily to do (i.e., check in somewhere, etc.) (FS25)

FS25 (a light user of the LBSN) is interesting in two ways. Initial interest is created through the "momentum" of the application, referring to the wider cultural environment in which technological news and development becomes part of everyday discourse and attracts usage from this environment. This is interesting as it indicates an understanding of technology and computer applications as an important part of the wider culture, but there is no indication here that this appreciation goes any further than the situating of mobile applications as a part of the cultural zeitgeist. The admission of not knowing what is being offered makes this lack of development (into world disclosing or understanding) clear. There is no indication that the process of checking-in is important in any way beyond itself, and contributes to the understanding of place. The device itself (and the LBSN) could be said to be orienting FS25 to do this (otherwise what is the point of having the service) and in this way, the check-in is a validation of downloading the application rather than an important part of the user's everyday experience.

There were many responses that indicated that checking-in is something that is done as a habitual behaviour,[1] without any reflection upon the place or the mediation of the computational device in locating oneself. These comments are characterised by check-ins being a way of "playing the game" of Foursquare:

> The points, badges and mayorships. It's like a little contest in our group. I'm disappointed when I forget to check in because I missed out on the points! (FS38)

> Well, mostly because I'm there and want to check in, especially if I plan on going there again, i.e. my house. You also get points for creating a location. Yay points! (FS38)

> Points! Like I said the video game achievement junkie reflex is kinda strong. Plus in some ways it's like being the first person to climb the mountain – I was there FIRST. (MS34)

The Foursquare LBSN obviously owes some of its popularity to the game aspect: the collecting of points and badges, and competing for "mayorships" of venues with other players is a key selling point. By focussing on this element, the place in which one checks-into is actively reduced to a resource for the accumulation of points or social capital (Ellison et al., 2011: 127) within the network, and the physical and social aspects of that place are ignored as the place is seen as something to be used in the accruement of credit. The technological understanding of the world and being is clear in these instances. A similar comment that reiterates the prevalence of this behaviour:

> Yes, there were "hot" places with many people checked in. And I myself got interested in those places as well. (FS50)

FS50 shows how the check-in facility influences the behaviour of users, in that this user cites that there were places that became of interest (or awareness) through others checking-in to that place. Again, there is no indication that the interest here is anything beyond the awareness of the place as somewhere within the network, as a place that could be used for social capital and as such reduced to resource.

The creation of a "place" within the database itself – that is, creating and then checking-in to a spot on Foursquare – was a behaviour that was commented on by some participants in the ethnography, and I want to place this kind of action in the technological revealing of location as it is indicative of using places and spaces as a resource within the culture of using LBSN and social networking:

> So that others who visit the spot can check-in too. (FS25)

FS25 offers an explanation of why users create places in Foursquare, again showing the possible reduction of place to resource, in this case as something that can be used by others in gaining points. This, too, accentuates the "screenic" nature of the understanding of place technologically through using LBSN, as a place must exist as part of the database in order for it to be meaningful, and as an entry in the database, it can be utilised as a check-in venue (for the accrual of points).

The actual performance of the behaviour of using the LBSN is interesting, as it offers some insight to the importance of the LBSN to users who do not consider it a vital part of their everyday lives. The following user offers an explanation of their behaviour in the context of the physical actions of the check-in and how it is a disruptive moment in what was previously automatic behaviour in visiting a new place.

> Since it could take a few minutes for the app to find me, the first thing I do when I get to a location is open the app so that I can get in before I get into the venue. There is a good chance the phone will not work when I'm inside a building. Besides, if I'm with my wife, she gets mad at me if I'm looking at the phone, so better to check in as I walk from the parking lot into the building. (MS0510201039)

Again, MS39 suggests that the behaviour is habitual and driven by the accruement of points and status (what is called gamification in the literature; see Bogost, 2011; Zichermann and Cunningham, 2011) but the idea here that others are bothered by the behaviour – yet still the behaviour is carried out, habitually – offers more evidence that the LBSN in some sense is a conditioning influence that prompts users to perform actions without reflecting on the place they are identifying with in a meaningful way. Similarly, MS56 also notes that the behaviour of using LSBN is socially constrained and controlled:

> As for family, I do check into places when I'm with them, but try to do it in a way that doesn't interrupt our conversation. I want to be respectful of my time with family. (MS56)

There is awareness from MS56 of the disruptive nature of the action and behaviour of using Foursquare. In speculating as to why some users differ in the extent to which Foursquare (and the computational device) offers a new disclosure of place, this notion of a disruptive moment could be important. The idea that the behaviour is disruptive in the context of the behaviours that one usually performs in everyday life may prevent the kind of instinctive, unconscious integration into everyday behaviour that may be necessary for an understanding of place to emerge. As it is, these users are using the LBSN to mark their own movements in the world – a form of self-monitoring and data production that can be used in the future. This kind of reflection on behaviour is not uncommon:

> If I like it or I'm waiting around with nothing happening, I check in. So my check-ins are either *bored* or *this is great*, or just peeing on a lamppost to mark my territory. (MS44)

> I also am more likely to check in if I'm bored, like waiting in doctor's office or something. (MS58)

MS44 and MS58 similarly see the application as a way of killing time, distracting themselves from the situation they are in and actively not engaging with the place in which they are situated. These responses can be linked to a notion of an inauthentic mode of existence, with the check-in being a kind of idle chatter that distracts the person from an appreciation of the place they inhabit, a distraction from concern (Malpas, 2000: 212).

A detailed comment offers more depth to the idea that using Foursquare as a behaviour can be commensurate with a technological mode of understanding places:

> A good example of this was I recently took a road trip with a friend to Sacramento from Ventura. Our goal that day was to get her the overshare badge and both of us as many points possible. It made the drive up more fun and I was checking Foursquare constantly for fun stuff to check into like "In A Car," which I am now the mayor of, Zombie Sheep Herd, etc. I was super pissed when the servers went down on our drive home. (FS38)

FS38 shows how she took a day of her life to earn a Foursquare badge, the "overshare" badge earned when one checks in to ten different places in 12 hours (Foursquare, 2011). The trip (the places, the time, where and what kind of place was visited) is not reflected upon, and there is exasperation when the process cannot be continued due to a technological failure. Moreover, FS38 takes pride in checking-into the car they are travelling in, a place that is mobile and I contend has been designated place only to earn the badge and points for the game. In this case, time, places and the everyday situation of being in a car are all reduced to resources for the furthering of the social capital of the person through gamification of location. On this theme, Bogost (2011) argues that *gamification is bullshit*, in that gamification is a technique used to coerce, conceal and impress as a sophisticated marketing technique to get users to use services. As such, the gamified service bears no relation to a game at all, but is a form of "exploitationware" pursued to capture a particular cultural moment.

Geo-location as a "technological" revealing of space

Geo-location refers to the application and interface of Foursquare itself, and how this application orients the user towards the world in a technological sense (that is, to reduce place to a resource to be used for social capital). There are three aspects that require attention: the gaming aspect of the interface (which I have already alluded to), the novelty of the experience, and the failure of Foursquare to meet the demands of some users, which in itself is interesting when considering the orientation and understanding of these users to the world and the service/device. These responses from the ethnography referred specifically to geo-location services and discussed the usage of applications and software directly, with the explicit aim of assessing how the application itself and its use effect the revealing of location for the user.

> Then the competition starts in, and the videogame "achievement junkie" bit kicks in. I've cut down a LOT on the use lately – some of that is the novelty is wearing off, and some is because I don't GO too many places that I'm not already mayor of. (MS34)

> It was an innovative and fun application to keep up with friends through friendly competition. (MS47)

MS34 and MS47 encapsulate the gaming aspect of Foursquare as an aspect of a technological understanding of place. Both respondents are previous users of Foursquare; they used the LBSN, but found it dull and decided to end use of the application. For both, the gaming aspect (which has been argued to constitute a reduction of place to resource) was the key driver for using the application, but the limited value of this in the long-term meant that the application has a limited appeal to the users. As MS34 states, if you do not go to many places, then that gaming aspect becomes old very quickly, as the value of the place is limited as a resource to be used. Once the resource is used up (and the novelty is gone) it is time to move on to something else. This comment reiterates that point:

> It became a competition among friends to maintain mayorship of our favourite bar for example. Creating new spots were incentivized by acquiring many additional points and thus being higher up on the weekly points leader stats. (MS47)

Again, MS47 is a lapsed user of the application (note the past tense of the comment) who reaffirms the idea that the competitive gaming aspect drove early use, but could not sustain attention or use of the application. Once the novelty of the game wears away (and the use of place as resource with it) then the application loses appeal. The following again reiterates the novelty aspect:

> I wanted to understand how it worked and enjoyed the novelty of the check-in experience. (MS51)

Here, the novelty of using the check-in itself is cited as a reason for using the application. A sense of curiosity motivated MS51, but that novelty could not hold their attention. This lack of engagement can be expressed as a desire for the new thing, a need to try something that becomes part of the cultural zeitgeist but that does not engage in a manner that has a transformative effect upon understanding of place because the user only treats the application as a way of deriving value from the place they locate themselves in at that time.

The idea of value, and of how Foursquare provides value for the user as a consumer is important. Rushkoff (in Silverman, 2011) has argued that thinking on the part of the user is confused as to what their status is in online spaces: while the user thinks they are the consumer, the consumer is actually the advertiser or investor in the service and the user is the product. The technological mode of understanding place goes some way to explaining this difficulty in subject position: the user believes they are deriving value from the application, while in reality the surplus value is derived from their activity to be sold as commodity (Marx,

1993: 134). This comment illustrates behaviour on the part of the user that leverages value from other sharing with other users:

> Originally none of my friends were on the service, and I managed to sign a few of them up to get more value out of Foursquare. (MS51)

MS51's response exemplifies the thinking that the user is consumer when using Foursquare. Following Rushkoff's argument, this could be due to a lack of awareness on the part of the user as to their role in such services, but the idea that the interface can act as a value generator for the individual ties up with the idea of a technological understanding neatly. In this sense, the user views the service, and other users, as resources to derive (social) capital from, and to be exploited as such. The idea of the application providing value is further supported by FE13's response:

> The only app in my opinion, which can be used to navigate the world is Yelp – I've planned nights out using the app because I wasn't an area I was familiar with. I've used Yelp in the past to plan a night out because I was in an area I didn't know very well. My choices were made on the number of stars for each venue and users comments. (FE13)

In the opinion of FE13, Foursquare lacks value as an application in comparison to Yelp (the utility coming from the perception and experience of using ratings on Yelp) hence it is not used.[2] Here, the interface of Foursquare is again seen as something from which value needs to be derived, indicative of a technological mode of understanding which does fundamentally distort the nature of the subject position that the user occupies in services like Foursquare.

Some participants in the ethnography expressed concerns with privacy and how usage is modified by these concerns. Certainly, privacy is a major focus of research with regard to LBSN,[3] and the concerns with sharing location do affect how one presents oneself to others. In particular, one female respondent from London expressed concerns about the possibility of sharing one's location and how the behaviour and practices of using LBSN are affected by considerations on privacy:

> I don't check in because I don't want folks to know where I am necessarily. I use twitter and Facebook to announce where I am if I think it's worthwhile saying something about it. Privacy is the other issue and we still don't have easy ways to manage this at a granular level. There are some people who I connect to on various services that sometimes,

it's ok to let them know where I am, and other times it's not. As a female, my default setting is to not let anyone know where I am. (FE06)

FE06 is expressing how "self-presentation" is a secondary concern to "self-preservation." It could be that the context of her usage (London) modifies the instinct to share, and reduces sharing. The concern expressed should not be explained away though, and this is a user that no longer uses the service based on these concerns. There is still though – in the comment "I use twitter and Facebook to announce where I am if I think it's worthwhile saying something about it" – a willingness to share location and benefit on a social level from identifying with a high-status place that will generate social capital when seen by others. Similar concerns with privacy were expressed by a number of male respondents:

> The fear that publically saying you are somewhere – means that strangers know where you are not! (MS63)

> Makes me think twice whether to "check in" or not? Just how much should be public … (MS63)

> I am aware when I send my location that I am telling anyone who might want to look that I am in a specific place or that I am away from my home. It is mostly an awareness of the safety of sending that information out. (MS23)

> No, but there are places I check in off the grid, so people don't know where I am. (MS59)

These comments augment the discussion on privacy, but all have a common theme that while privacy is acknowledged and valued, it is a modifying factor in checking-in and sharing that data, rather than an absolute barrier. There is also a commonality that all the respondents are male, an interesting gender perspective that privacy, personal safety and the protection of property are concerns for male users that were not reported (although it is not within the scope of this analysis to conclude not considered) by females. The possibility and realisation of value through associating oneself with a place of high social status can supersede such concerns. The notion of sharing location as a means of generating interest from others is something that has been commented upon by other respondents. Interestingly, there is some evidence of location-sharing as socially negative, in that such data is not viewed positively:

> They didn't see the relevance. At least three people commented on separate occasions something to the effect of "huh?" or "so?"

I guess Facebook status updates would make more sense in the context of "I've just been to Wetherspoons to have breakfast with the family" as opposed to just Checked In to Wetherspoons. (ME02)

I only share my check-ins with my foursquare friends, half of which I don't particularly know other than that they've been mayors of places I've checked into. I tried sharing my check-ins with Facebook but most of my friends thought the idea of me sharing everywhere I've been a little odd. (ME02)

I specifically avoid posting my Foursquare updates to other social networks (such as Twitter) as I am aware of how many of my friends on the other networks would consider this "spamming" the timeline, which might negatively affect me on those networks. (ME04)

Often they will laugh at me, rolling their eyes if they see me checking in, and asking me why I bother. (MS31)

Time, interest level in the location, e.g. do I think my network will be interested. (MS33)

One may want to share location in one social network, but would avoid doing this in another to avoid negative social consequences from other users. This group of comments are important as they position location sharing within the context of other media services and social networking tools, and how management of self-image and self-presentation is managed in a multi-platform way. Again, this reiterates the view of a technological mode of revealing on the part of users, as place is not just reduced to commodity or data, but is also rejected as socially valuable by the presentation of place as a commodity of worth. In this sense, place has a market value that is not worth sharing in the existing social networks that people use and are part of, and if this is the case, then information is not shared to preserve the social capital that the individual has within that network. It is again worth noting that all the respondents in these examples are males, and that the concern for place as a commodity that provides social value is something that was expressed clearly by male participants and was not an *expressed* concern of female participants, although this gender difference would require further investigation before any conclusion could be confidently expressed.

A key element of these user responses is that to an extent, the use of their devices in their everyday lives corresponds to this *pessimistic view of how humans can become dependent upon such devices.* These users are reflexive about their own involvement in a reduction of their identity and use of space as resource (specifically social capital), rather than developing an appreciation of place using the technology available. I conclude this section with a declarative statement from a London-based user.

> If by "social identity" you are referring to the profile that I use to interact with my friends and family online, to share photos, what I am doing, status updates, engage in a conversation, etc., then at this point in time, there is no effective way to manage social identity online because it is either all or nothing – either to reveal your everyday activities online completely (via location disclosure) or not at all. (ME08)

I feel that ME08 is correct in respect to how managing the image of self is related to different understandings of the world, either technological or computational. An all-in approach may be indicative of a computational orientation to the world, and this will be explored in the next chapter. Management of identity is, however, difficult, and in these cases is often reduced to a commoditisation of place and self in order to maximise social capital.

One respondent made a number of comments on the nature of the relationship between user and device that illustrate a technological mode of revealing. It should be noted that this respondent is a heavy Foursquare user and these comments are extracted in isolation from some other comments that were made, which were indicative of a modern or technological revealing of place. These comments were coded in the macro-analysis following the close reading of the data as *independence*, as the comments were unique in positioning the device and LBSN purely as a resource to be used, with no value beyond that position.

> It is just a tool on your hand and is faster to get information specially if you are on the road. (MS36)

Although this is an isolated comment in the context of this ethnography, the point is important enough to be raised: if the device is seen only as a tool for moving efficiently from point A to point B, then the function of the device is to reduce territory or space to the level of data, which is not something commensurate with a poetic revealing of place.

Management of self-image as a technological orientation to the device

In considering management of self-image, the focus is on use of Foursquare as a way of presenting an image of the user to others in a particular manner. The key to understanding this presentation in this argument is whether this is indicative of a technological mode of understanding place. If the management of place were commoditised or leveraged for the production of social capital then this would be indicative of such an understanding. The user comments analysed in this section are all indicative of managing self-image and leveraging social capital from Foursquare use, positioning the revealing of location in the use of the LBSN as technological (location as a resource):

> I'm not overly concerned about my image but I do check in more often if I'm somewhere and I want people to know I'm there (like at a concert, skiing at Lake Tahoe, visiting a hip restaurant, or when I'm in Hawaii). I avoid checking in to my home, work or boring places. I check into the gym so I can go on record that I worked out. (FE16)

> I would not check in places like the doctor's office. The only exception is I'm pregnant and the next appointment we can find out if we're having a boy or girl. So I will check in and let people know when I find out. (FE16)

These responses are indicative of many in the ethnography. A user will check-into high-status venues or places that can be commented upon in a positive light by others, generating social capital from others based on the sharing of this location. While one may not be working out at the gym even though there is a check-in for the venue, the implication of activity can be enough for social capital. There is a clear implication that the place one checks-into is somewhere that can be used to derive capital for the individual, and this consideration of place as something that can be used to increase personal capital. This conclusion is also consistent with using the application as a means of monitoring self and producing data on oneself for self-monitoring purposes. The following comments show similar usage:

> Also I like to let others know about what places I like to go do. (FS30)

> So I could find friends on the go and vice versa. (FS49)

To keep track of my moving history (FS50)

To kind of map out where I go throughout the day. (FS55)

I like to keep people up-to-date with my daily goings-on and I've been told by friends that they like to see what I'm up to since I don't talk to them daily. (FS0610201055)

An initial observation on these responses is that all are made by females; the need and drive for self-surveillance could be a gender-specific issue, and while such an analysis is beyond the scope of this project, the identification of this tendency amongst female participants could be the basis for further analysis in future research, particularly given the dominance of research on issues regarding privacy in the literature. This notion of self-surveillance is interesting in that not only does it fit with a technological mode of understanding the world, but it also shows how the stream of information that is produced by using computational devices and applications in everyday life contributes back to the understanding of one's place in the world. Here, there are elements of sousveillance (see Mann et al., 2002; Michael and Michael, 2012) in that the ubiquitous device collects information on the everyday actions and motions of the user and this can be spread across social networks seamlessly (but with the consent of the user in this case). Berry (2012c) talks about self-monitoring as a form of life-stream or quantified-self (see Berry, 2012c). The reduction of place to consumable information is the presentation of place facilitated by computational devices – the orientation of the user to place and device is one that sees the device as a "coded object" for the production of data, rather than understanding place (Berry, 2012b). It is the idea that location can be presented (see FS55) to others for their consumption that still makes this a set of observations that correspond to the technological mode of understanding. It is that this information is not just for self-understanding, but also promotes the self and commoditises the everyday behaviours that one performs that suggests a technological mode of understanding place. The idea that one promotes and shares location to produce social capital is supported by a number of other responses, such as:

I have some ground rules regarding my check-ins – no private homes unless there's a party or a social gathering (my friend opened a venue for my house, and my girlfriend is the mayor), no cities nor little streets. (ME09)

The idea that checking-in is rule based, and those rules derive from principles that are commensurate with the production of social capital due to association with high-status venues, reiterates the point that there is a technological mode of understanding place at work that reduces place to commodity to be associated with and to derive benefit from checking-in. The distribution of such high-status check-ins is also acknowledged:

> I'm pretty aware of the image I put out using 4sq and Twitter. I will confess that if my friends saw me check in to burger places all the time, I probably wouldn't hear the end of it. (ME15)

ME15 recognises that the check-in will affect how others treat the person within the context of the information provided by the service. Self-presentation in the context of data therefore becomes a vital aspect of self-management, and this again is commensurate with the technological mode of being, in that the presentation of oneself is modified to maximise one's social capital and place is reduced to resource to facilitate the maximum value of this self-presentation. The following comments reiterate this analysis:

> Some other places I want to make sure that everyone knows where I am. Sometimes a check in is a badge of honour. (ME03)

> I may decline to check-in to some locations because it's out of context or I don't consider it as of interest to my friends. (ME14)

> I don't check into shops because its boring and I have nothing really to say about shops, I don't always check into railway stations because it's a bit dull unless I'm going to see a client. (MP20)

> It was also a good way to let people know you were going out and where to go on a given night. (MS47)

> Depending on the location, there is some sense of value in the recognition by others. (MS54)

> I do it most often when I want to publicize where I am so others can join me or at least be aware. (MS58)

Check-ins act as a source of value and capital for the individual in the context of how they present themselves to others. It is also worth noting that in these replies all the respondents are male. This observation must be considered within the conclusion that overwhelmingly in this ethnography, there is recognition that locating oneself and identifying with place produces information that *has a value when shared with others in a social network,* and hence such activity is consciously monitored by the user to produce such an effect that is beneficial – an interesting computational feedback loop (see Berry, 2012c).

The technological revealing of space as resource

This chapter has proposed that there is a technological orientation to place that arises from particular motivations for using LBSN that frames and orients the user to understand space as resource to be used. Certain responses illustrate this orientation, where comments were indicative of physical space being reduced to a resource to be used in the future for the user:

> I'll create spots for places that I frequent, once again, to journal the places I go. (MS61)

> Trending venues is also interesting. I mostly only care where my friends check-in, though. Don't care so much about strangers. (FE1906201164)

Here, place is something to be created or taken note of only if it is popular. The idea that if a place is outside the database of places then it has no use or value is indicative of the technological mode of understanding places, in that if the place is not inscribed into the Foursquare database then there is no way that one can extract value from that place. This would be consistent with viewing the service as an extension of a worldview where all things are to be considered a resource.

An interesting set of comments contend that Foursquare – as a service – is not something that is useful in finding places, and therefore does not effectively differentiate place (i.e. a location meaningful to people) from space (the physical environment).

> Not specifically – generally I am only aware of and check in to locations that I am already aware of. (ME04)

> Generally, the use of Foursquare or Gowalla has not increased my awareness of places around me. (ME08)

In these comments, it is clear that there is an intention to utilise the service to find new places, but that the service has failed in this task. In both cases this cannot be attributed to a weak technological infrastructure (both respondents are based in large British urban conurbations). The following comment facilitates this analysis:

> I find it's inaccurate and tells me little about what's going on around me or places to go. With the exception of Google maps and Nokia maps on my mobile, I would say that LBSN is something I actively *don't* use because it adds little or no value to the existing ways I find out about stuff going on around me. (FE06)

The comment by FE06 suggests an inability on the part of the interface and application to replace pre-existing sources of knowledge, and this inability limits the extent to which usage can challenge the world understanding of technicity (of all things to be used as resource). The user cannot gain value from the device, and so does not use the device and LBSN as there is no perceived need to use the device in comparison with other devices.

> Foursquare's interface is not well suited to specific searches by type of place or even for nearby venues (seems to get proximity wrong a lot and miss tons of key places). I was hoping that Foursquare would provide richer understanding of places I am in. Other than finding a hidden washroom at a subway station I frequent, this generally has not happened. Most of the comments on place are quite superficial, well known, or narcissistic. (ME05)

ME05's comment complements this analysis. Although the interface has been modified with an "explore" feature since this comment, which allows a linking of current location with similar locations in the locale, the perception of the interface being unable to meet the task of effectively finding new places obviously limits the possibility of understanding places based on usage. From this failure, the user perceived the majority of usage on Foursquare as not revealing place at all, but as a series of narcissistic statements on personal location that would seem to relate to this discussion of the reduction of place to resource for social capital and hence reinforce a technological mode of revealing location.

Technological revealing of the world

In this chapter, the technological understanding of places has been positioned as a normative ontotheology (a dominant theory or position taken as truth) that is the dominant mode of understanding space in the modern world. Users, in many cases, express that using the technology hasn't changed their experience of the world, but as the responses of users have shown, the way in which they negotiate space, particular unfamiliar spaces, is transformed when connected to LBSN. For example FE13 claims in a comment:

> I wouldn't go as far as saying that it has changed my perception of the world. (FE13)

This chapter has provided an analysis of LBSN use that exemplifies how particular usage of devices and LBSN results in an understanding of venues as resources, rather than places that are both meaningful in themselves and allow for an attunement to place. This effect is not confined to the revealing of the venue as resource, but also the revealing of entities in that venue (including other people) as resource also. The practices indicative of this understanding are not only the usage of the device to ascertain which venues have most "value," as this would indicate that the device alone is responsible for a technological understanding of place. The orientation of the user to the world, as a person that seeks to maximise the value of their location in the context of the social capital that could be accrued from locating oneself in a particular place, is what directs usage of the LBSN and device as part of this technological understanding. The use of Foursquare as a means to accrue social capital corresponds to a technological revealing in that location is used as resource. The meaningful relationship to place described in Chapter 4 is replaced with a view of location as somewhere that can be leveraged through connectivity to social networks and LBSN to manage self-presentation or improve social capital. This technological revealing is not of place as a referential totality or meaningful existential locale. Location is meaningful in these examples only as far as it can improve perception of the user to others, rather than be experienced as a place with a meaningful impact on the user through their presence there and the use of LBSN to understand that location.

The understanding of place that was explored in Chapter 5 that comes from the use of LBSN as a way of gathering important information for understanding place *as* place is an alternative to the usage and practices identified in this chapter. However, these practices come from the same people; the desire to understand place as a meaningful locale and as a resource to be shared both emerge from a desire to understand the world, but are *different in both practices of use and orientation to the world*. As such, the same user can reveal physical space as space or place at different times, given a change in their orientation to the world at different times or a change in the usage of the device at different times, in particular if the place being understood is meaningful beyond social capital. In this chapter, the desire for understanding the world that is a part of the technological worldview is part of a desire to value and commoditise space for social capital, a "screenic" use of the technology that presents places as venues to be utilised through mediated presence that assists in the accrual of this capital; the alternate to the orientation and the practices of use that exemplify that orientation towards place explored in Chapter 5. The phenomenological implications – how this affects the lived-in experience of place and how the presence of the device and LBSN plays a role in this altering appreciation of place – of this dual appreciation and varying orientation to place are critical in relating back to the importance of Martin Heidegger in the digital post-phenomenology of place. While devices are embodied and actions take place in a computationally-infused environment thanks to code, the mood of the user is still critical to the kind of understanding of place that will be experienced.

7
Conclusions

This book has proposed a *digital post-phenomenology of place* or *post-Heideggerian phenomenology* where the key notions of placehood in Heidegger's work (care, attunement, situatedness) are embodied in practices to attune to an information-infused world. These are all necessary conditions for the *feeling* of place, but no single one is sufficient; the *digital post-phenomenology* requires a particular mood or towards-which and situatedness, and the condition of a computational environment for this kind of attunement and understanding of place. In the ethnography, mood was found to be the critical element, as users revealed place technologically or dwelled with technology in a Sloterdijkian sphere to reveal place as *place* poetically. This awareness of place is dwelling (Crandall, 2011: 50). These world-revealing moments arise as users use the device and LBSN in their lives as a means of moving through and navigating the world and the device becomes a focal point for practices in the average everydayness of the user. As a final comment from the ethnography, consider the following:

> I know that my friends frequent a certain place even though I've never bumped into them there. (FS0510201030)

The use of LBSN allows this user to know where their friends are. In making this comment, the user's knowledge of their friends location – in real-time – means that they are aware of the social experiences of their friends and have an idea of what occurs in that place despite not "being there" at that time. This is an important aspect of digital being-with that is influenced by the streaming of location information through the LBSN. In doing this, the user is comported towards understanding events in the world through the information provided by the LBSN. Attunement to the digital world through the embodied use of digital devices affords the possibility of this worlding. Additionally, the presence of code and computation as a foregrounding to the use of computational technology is necessary, as conceptualised through Sloterdijk's foam.

The user uses the LBSN to make sense of events and place, and to gain insight into the activities of others above and beyond speculating about what is happening or reading an account after the event. The role of the real-time data-stream that the LBSN (and many other computer-mediated communication mediums) generates is important in the revealing of place. It is embodied practices of use that are critical to linking to these, but the code of the application links us to this plethora of information that is used in understanding place through contribution and use for navigation.

This book has from the outset argued that the understanding of space and place are two different phenomenological conceptions of the same physical region, and from within a software studies approach the presence of computational devices, code, software, data and information has a critical role in mediating between these two understandings as co-constituents of place (with orientation and embodiment). The poetic revealing of place is a revealing of place where place is allowed to come forth from a letting-come-forth. The orientation of the person to the physical region and the arrangement of things in that region are critical to how a phenomenal, lived-in place is differentiated from pure physical space, and it has been argued (following Heidegger's analysis of tools in *Being and Time*) that interaction with equipment (such as computational devices) is critical to orientation. These interactions are embodied, embodiment is critical to dwelling, and attunement to the digital world is co-constitutive, involving being-there, embodied action, device, software and connectivity.

The orientation to place is two-fold, in that it is not only a doing-with tools that allows place to be revealed, but also the pre-interaction towards-which that is important as part of a co-construction of place or understanding of place that is contingent on the practices of using the device and LBSN and being in a mood or orientation to place that seeks understanding as place rather than utilisable space. By this, I have argued that the orientation of the person towards tools is important in how the person projects themselves forwards in their interaction with equipment.

This kind of revealing of place is dependent not only on the tool and the arrangement of the tool in the world[1] but also the intentions of the user and their reasons for using LBSN at the time they are using it. The intentions or reasons for usage are important in how the user regards the device and how the device as a thing gathers the user into the event of world-revealing. In the discussion of the ethnography the practices of use that are towards being-with other people (sharing location with other people with a social intention as opposed to the intention of accruing social capital) and towards understanding place as relative to the user and through the impressions formed by other users were the intentions that were seen as common in what was identified as a poetic or modern revealing of place.

This stood in contrast to the towards-which of accruing social capital and the game elements of the LBSN that were identified as part of the technological revealing of place when using LBSN. The being-towards revealing place is afforded by the code of LBSN, which organises and gathers the elements of the world (as understood in the fourfold) through the encoding of location and socially meaningful information and gazetteers and allows for the revealing of place through this gathering, of which the being-towards understanding place is a part. Even though code is withdrawn from the conspicuous awareness of the user, it shapes the experience of place through its gathering of key semantically meaningful elements of place and as such projects a processual agency of computational code for the revealing of place poetically, that is as a letting-come-forth of place.

The being-at-home with technology that is identified as important in the revealing of place is the embodied attunement that one has to not only the device but also the place in the locating of oneself at the place through using the device. The practice of checking-into a place or exploring the opinions of others at a place are how the tool is used in the process of locating oneself at the place, but the revealing of the place as a place is also through the intention or towards-which of the user. When thinking of this in the context of Heidegger's fourfold, the check-in and using of LBSN is the ground, the towards-which the skies or future paths that emerge from the usage of the device and the towards-which orientation to the device, the mortals the user, and the divinity the being-at-home with technology and the worldhood (or indeed placehood) that is the attunement to place that comes from the use of the device in this manner.

This kind of focal practice of using LBSN is what has been identified as part of the event of revealing place. This is not the entire event though; the attunement to place is the product of the gathering of the thing that depends on the orientation to the device and practice of use. This attunement is the being-at-home with LBSN; it is the dwelling-with

LBSN. When man dwells,[2] a local world is created that allows for things to come forth as a letting-come-forth rather than being-stood-forth in a technological revealing. This poetic revealing from the gathering of the fourfold by the thing is in essence the understanding of place; man understands place as things standing in relation to one another in a referential totality, but this revealing is only possible if man is attuned to the local world of the thing and not challenging the location as resource.

The identification of the practices and intentions or towards-which of users that characterise technological and modern (or poetic) revealing of place using LBSN stand as the original contribution to scholarship of this book, along with the explicit linking of the care structure of *Being and Time* as the entry point to the event of world-disclosure or *Ereignis* in the later Heidegger. It is important to clarify what exactly *place* means in light of this analysis. By place, I am referring to the clearing (*Lichtung*) that is opened up by the event of world-disclosing, and how this cleared place is different to the spatial understanding that is the product of the technological revealing and the understanding of space that I characterised with the spatial theories of Descartes and Newton in the introduction to this thesis.

In this view, place is not a conception of space as physical co-ordinate and the relation between things as physical entities, but is the emergent phenomena that that is the product of man's taking of things into care and engagement with things as meaningful entities in themselves rather than physical bodies (objects) in space. Place is the local world or existential locale that comes from the engagement with things, but, as was argued in Chapter 3, this is not a product of man's (or Dasein's) projection of meaning onto regions of space, but is explicitly a phenomenon that arises from the towards-which of Dasein, the taking of a thing into care, the "thinging" of the thing (the gathering of the person, practices, towards-which and mood of the user) and the event of world-disclosure that reveals place as place to the user of the thing. The "thinging" of the thing makes the local world possible, but this is contingent upon the towards-which of Dasein and the manner of engagement of Dasein with the thing. The event of the world-disclosure (and the revealing of the place as place) is in this view a hermeneutic event, where the constituent parts of the event are not sufficient to reveal the phenomenological entirety of the event, but are necessary for the emergence of this event that should be understood as the understanding of place as place and not space. Place should be understood as the phenomenological realisation of the referential totality of entities as a mood of Dasein (the dwelling of Dasein) that can only be poetic in its revealing, and the constituent elements of the event are understood in the context of the event as a revealing of place rather than as individually realised elements in isolation from one another. The revealing and realisation of place is therefore hermeneutic, rather than physical or spatial.

This corresponds to what Malpas (2008: 1) calls Heidegger's "topology" of being, place and world. Place sits centrally in this topology, linking the core philosophical issues of *Being and Time* (care, the transcendental Dasein, and the ground of being) to issues of unity (world and worldhood) in the later Heidegger (Malpas, 2008: 2). By using the term topology Malpas is clearly making the study of place central to understanding the entirety of Heidegger's project, and place as the middle term in what Malpas considers the three totemic themes in Heidegger's work again indicates the centrality of place to Heidegger's philosophy when viewed a as body of work hermeneutically. Place, when understood as the world-revealing event or clearing that sweeps away ontotheology and makes entities visible as things in themselves in a referential totality, is part of the being of Dasein in-the-world and of the world itself. When Heidegger argues that "The authentic relation of the world and Dasein is care and meaningfulness" (Heidegger, 1992: 221), the care and meaningfulness in this view is place, as place links Dasein and world and is, in the view proposed in this book, dependent upon Dasein's bringing of things into both care and meaningfulness through the towards-which that Dasein encounters things with prior to the event.

It should be noted that in Dasein's average everydayness, and overwhelmingly in the ethnography constructed to provide evidence for the central research questions of this thesis, the world (and therefore space and place) is revealed through a technological revealing. This totalising ontotheology is noted in not just some respondents, but all; those respondents whose comments were interpreted as revealing place through the use of LBSN also offered replies consistent with a technological revealing of place as space that can be used as resource. That there was some evidence that this revealing can be challenged by a series of practices and orientations to the world is positive in light of the research questions and theoretical position of this book, but the marginal nature of these practices illustrates an important point about the revealing of place. This is not an inevitable consequence of everyday life (and certainly not of using LBSN) and the everyday understanding of place should be considered consistent with the technological world-disclosure.

The focal practices and motivations of users therefore play a major role in how users encounter the device, take it into care, create a local world through the moment of using the device to locate themselves and are gathered by the thing into the event that is a place for understanding place itself. The ethnography aimed to identify what practices and focuses are responsible for technological or modern revealing of place, or how users take the device and LBSN into care in such a manner that the dwelling attunement to world occurs. Using the device to anticipate and locate others within a community of LBSN users, actively using the device to locate oneself in a novel space and understand that space as a set of places of interest and using the device as an everyday part of one's life for understanding place are the focal practices that allow for the letting-come-forth of place through the device's "thinging". These key marginal practices of use allow for place to come forth rather than space being stood-forth as a challenge to be mastered.

The poetic revealing is marginal in that it is in opposition to the totalising ontotheology of technological revealing. The totalising of the technological worldview is expressed in Heidegger's philosophy as a change in ontotheology. The root of the word ontotheology derives from considerations of the ontology of God and the theology of being and was first used in the modern era by Immanuel Kant, differentiating ontotheology from cosmotheology as two kinds of transcendental theology (Thomson, 2005: 7). Heidegger's use of the term encompasses the whole of metaphysics, or metaphysical theories, and is used to argue that metaphysical theories ground our understanding of "what is" in every age (Thomson, 2005: 9). This notion of securing an epoch (Thompson, 2005: 2) draws a relationship between Heidegger and Nietzsche, and links Heidegger's idiosyncratic understanding of metaphysics with his consideration of Nietzsche as "the end of metaphysics," with the will to power being the absolute final position of metaphysics, a "will to will" (Lozar, 2008: 121) that only recognises the selfish interests of mankind (Heidegger, 1977: 93). That metaphysics grounds an age (Heidegger, 1977: 115) means that it guides our comportment towards things and therefore enframing is a kind of grounding that is made possible by the presence of technology.[3]

With regard to technology, it is Nietzsche's "unthought" that is responsible for our nihilistic technological understanding of the being of entities. Although Nietzsche was motivated by a need to avoid nihilism, the understanding of being as an eternally recurring will to power encourages the understanding of all entities, including ourselves, as *Bestand*, resources standing by to be optimised (Thomson, 2005: 44). Heidegger's understanding of our age derives from his understanding of metaphysics as ontotheology – a hermeneutic connection – and specifically from

Nietzsche's metaphysic that removes the ontological anchoring of metaphysics to ground. This technological mode of being produces a "calculative thinking" that quantifies all relations and entities to programmable information (Heidegger, 1998b: 139), and this becomes more pervasive as it avoids our gaze. The danger of technology is therefore the entrenchment of this ontotheology as the totalising of the ontotheology (that is, driving out all other modes of revealing) that results in a forgetting of being itself.[4] The poetic revealing can be read as a reaction to this ontotheology that results from an orientation to the world that seeks to include other entities in thinking about location and place rather than to reduce those entities to resource.

This research has aimed to avoid ahistorical criticism through acknowledging the importance of computational code in the poetic revealing of place as well as its role in ordering a technological revealing; this acknowledgement also addresses the one-dimensional criticism Feenberg (2003) makes of Heidegger's critique. This has been done by outlining a description of the non-technological understanding of place and how entities are positioned within that world (or worlds) in relation to other entities. Heidegger was happy to forego discussions on specific technologies, as the essence of modern technology would necessarily be the same no matter what form or function that technology took. In this book, computational devices have been conceptualised as devices that through their use of code can order and arrange information and practices that provide the sufficient conditions for a poetic revealing of place. Allied to a mood or orientation to the world that seeks an understanding of place rather than space, the revealing of place is achievable through using computational devices and LBSN in the marginal practices of disclosing location and place as a product of taking the device into care. If this is the case, the world will not be revealed technologically, and an understanding of place will be one that takes things into care and reveals through the equipmental spatiality that allows for a revealing of place, as a referential totality of things, that is meaningful through the orientation of Dasein to those things as a non-enframed attunement to place. The evidence from users of Foursquare in this book is that there is the possibility of a revealing of place as a meaningful existential locale if there is an appropriate orientation to the world that is rooted in a taking of computational devices into everyday activity and a mood or desire to understand place as a locale with deeper meaning than mere co-ordinates to be used in the execution of goals.

The findings on how one may reveal place through the use of the device and LBSN does lead to the possibility of an accusation of techno-fetishism or a technologically determinist stance and, with this being one of Feenberg's (1999) key criticisms of Heidegger's critique of technology, this does require a defence. Techno-fetishism here refers to the users that experience a poetic revealing of place and situate their own use of LBSN within the wider personal use of digital applications and computational devices in everyday life. This can be read as advocating that the only method of achieving a poetic or modern revealing of place is through the adoption of these wider computational practices in everyday life. As such, this is open to the criticism of technological determinism in that the average everyday life of a user must include the use of computational devices in order to achieve the revealing of place that has been advocated as superior to the technological revealing of place in this book.[5] This is problematic in that it leads to a seeming contradiction-in-terms; one can only break free of the technological revealing of place if one gives oneself over to using technology as an essential part of everyday living.

The problematic aspect of this can of course be answered succinctly in the assertion from Heidegger's own critique of technology that *the essence of technology is nothing technological* (Heidegger, 1977: 35). The use of the device to reveal place poetically is as a thing, not as an exclusively technological artefact. That the computational device may not reveal technologically is hardly contradictory to the view of this research or necessarily to the views of Heidegger in his later philosophy. However, there is in this work a pattern: that those users that show evidence of using LBSN in a manner that allows for a revealing of place poetically are enthusiastic users of technology in everyday life, and early adopters of technology such as social networking, smartphones and LBSN.

As this is the case, the idea that the poetic revealing is only possible in an average everydayness dominated by technology is a concern. There are two responses to this that are important to consider. Firstly, the idea of the everyday life in which technology is a stable companion (a being-with technology) should not necessarily be seen as inevitable, but neither should it be seen as undesirable. The main desire to explore the questions of this research was because of the increased use of smartphones and computational devices in everyday life, and because these devices are becoming more integrated in the lives of more people daily. The rationale for this research not only predicted this but also observed it as a daily phenomenon that was worthy of research. While this phenomenon is in itself marginal at this time, that is no reason to suggest that this will not become a more normal mode of existence as time progresses – as William Gibson (1999) argues, "the future has already arrived. It's just not evenly distributed yet."

Secondly, the technological mode of world-disclosure can be explained by this problem in a parsimonious way. If a tension between the use of computational devices and non-computational methods to situate oneself in the world results in a use of LBSN that is consistent with the technological mode of revealing, then this offers an explanation for the prevalence of the technological mode of revealing in the responses in the ethnography. The mixed use of non-computational and computational methods and practices in everyday life may be indicative of the inability to dwell with LBSN through hesitancy in taking the application into *care* by the presence of other, more trusted or accustomed means of locating oneself and understanding place that is non-computational. If this is so, then one might expect more people to report a poetic revealing of place in the future if the uptake of LBSN continues to rise amongst people that use computational devices frequently or take computational methods into their average everydayness as an expected and ordinary part of their everyday life. In responding to the original criticism raised, there is neither a techno-fetishism nor technological determinism being advocated in this work; there is a possible reading that suggests that the position the user must be in to experience a revealing of place must be dependent upon a cultural frame of everyday life where computational technology dominates everyday practice. Alternatively, it is proposed that these computational practices are not dominant (or determining) but are taken up in the towards-which of the person in their average everydayness; and a towards-which or orientation to the device that sees such technology as adjacent to or purely supplemental to the other everyday practices of location or understanding of place may be part of the technological mode of revealing, as LBSNs are another way to leverage resources from space.

The use of the ethnographic method, while justified in Chapter 5, is in itself admittedly problematic in establishing these conclusions, as the method is highly subjective in analysis; moreover the use of hermeneutic phenomenological analysis as a means of analysing responses is particularly subjective. While the theoretical position of this exploration was established in Chapters 3 to 4, the choice of research methods in this thesis does leave the work open to the charge of subjectivity. This research is not intended to be read solely as an empirical, descriptive work, but as a critical and theoretical contribution. While the empirical research on LBSN has value, this research looks to understand LBSN use through a critical perspective and therefore has a set of methods necessarily different to those in the empirical field. It could be argued that phenomenological research is not something that lends itself at all to empirical research, which is why this could be termed quasi-empirical in that the aim of the ethnography was to legitimise the theoretical position and test the research questions as hypotheses but without explicitly empirical methods, which in themselves would not offer an insight into the phenomenological, lived-in experience of using LBSN.

Gamification, Foursquare and the future

Bogost (2011) has argued that gamification is an exploitative marketing technique designed to capitalise on a cultural moment. This capitalisation of use (and users) of LBSN can be explained with reference to the political economy of LBSN, and it is this capitalisation of use that is a possible barrier to a revealing of place through LBSN. This book has bracketed political economic questions due to restrictions in scope and length, though it is interesting that Smythe (2006) would probably argue that the gamified LBSN itself is something that transforms the user into a commodity that pays for the free usage of the service with labour, in the construction of the database of places.

It is interesting to note that Foursquare's own application is now moving away from a game/database creation model into a navigation model that aims to add value to user experiences through the use of the application in the world with the addition of an "explore" function into the application architecture (Foursquare, 2012). On 23 July 2014, Foursquare emailed the first 500,000 users of the service (from, now, over 50,000,000 users) to announce that check-ins would be now be done on a new application called "Swarm" while the rebranded Foursquare would represent the following:

> This is the beginning of the "personalized local search" future we've been talking about since we started Foursquare. It's been built with the help of our amazing 50,000,000-strong community, with all your tips, check-ins, photos, and the smarts we layered on top of that. You've been with us for a while, and all of your check-ins and history will continue to help shape your recommendations. (Foursquare, 2014)

The gamification aspect therefore seems to be waning as the "work" of constructing the database itself is now at a stage where such an explore feature could be implemented and be useful to users. When this research was conducted in 2011, gamification was seen by users as important in using the application: it is now seen as of so little importance that this aspect has been siphoned off into its own application. The design of applications that build gamification into their data collection procedures should be viewed critically in terms of political economy, but the comments in the ethnography are also important in that users that reported that they stopped using the service or became bored of it often cited a loss of novelty of this gamification aspect, and users that reported revealing of place through LBSN use rarely reported the gamification aspect at all in their usage. If there is a desire to design applications that aim for an understanding of place beyond the commoditised and gamification-led model, then the design of the application should look towards a sharing of social gazetteers and user experiences with a sharing of location to specified user groups defined by the user rather that the commoditisation of place and user.[6]

While this is what Foursquare has done, this is a "catch-22" recommendation in many ways, as getting users to take up the service in the first place does require a feature that will draw users in, and undoubtedly in the case of Foursquare the gamification model was critical to this initial use of the application.[7] After five years, this is no longer needed and Foursquare is now an application for navigation. The building of a database of millions of recommendations, spots and check-ins has created the necessary library for navigating, and anticipates perhaps what is to come next with technology in the digital milieu. As we stand on the precipice of wearable technology, the check-in and manual searching become passé embodied practices. If one has a location-enabled smartwatch, glasses or clothes then the recommendations on place one receives will need to be through an interface that provides information instantly and contextually. The harvesting of our social media and computational histories to provide context- and person-specific information in real-time will be the mechanism to provide this information.

As such, the research in this book may well be passé as soon as it is on the page, to borrow from Jason Farman. The historical moment of Foursquare, LBSN in the form of Foursquare or similar applications and the haptic, embodied use of mobile devices is coming to a close and the notion of marking location, sharing location and understanding location as place in this manner will be historical. However, the new technologies will still need a phenomenological framework to understand the subjective experience of place that they co-constitute. The mood or orientation of the user will remain, the technology will be embodied in new but always necessary ways and the environment will be more infused with information and data to use in understanding and orienting to place. Personal information will still be pushed over social networks for prestige and stored in databanks for aggregation and use. As the digital world is here to stay, location-based technology and services will become more important than ever in delivering contextualised information to users to navigate the world. As these technologies become more intimate we will still address them in a particular mood and orient ourselves to place in a particular way through using the information according to mood, as the framework here argues.

Notes

1 Introduction

1. These devices include Global Positioning Technology as standard, a link to a system of 24 satellites orbiting the planet that through a process of triangulation can determine the position of the device on the planet.
2. Gamification is the use of game mechanics and game-thinking to solve problems and engage audiences (Zichermann and Cunningham, 2011: ii).
3. Foursquare uses a game-based LBSN architecture, where users are awarded points for check-ins to places and compete with other users on a leaderboard. Points are awarded for checking in to a place, creating a place and for being in the same place or category of place for consecutive weeks. If a user has more check-ins than all others to a particular place, they are awarded the status of "mayor" of that place.
4. Infamously, Descartes denied the possibility of a vacuum.
5. The point of connection between the extended and the un-extended was not satisfactorily explained in Descartes philosophy, and essentially became the mind-body problem in philosophy.
6. Cognitive map is a very popular term in psychology that literally refers to a map in the mind. (Kitchin, 1994) "Cognitive maps: what are they and why study them?" *Journal of Environmental Psychology*, 14: 1–19.
7. Coyne (2010: i) calls this a tuning to place, and argues that this comes from incremental adjustments within spaces. What Coyne considers incremental adjustments using social media and ubiquitous computing can be understood as a set of practices that when attuned to other people and the space itself become world-revealing, and hence key to understanding space through how they allow the world to be revealed in an unforced, non-instrumental manner.

2 A (Brief) History of Understanding Space and Place

1. This lack of cartographic reason (Crampton, 2009: 1) can be explained as a result of the lack of ontotheology at the time; the clearing operating without the obscuring of metaphysics.
2. That is, world for Heidegger – the existential locale of Dasein where things stand in a referential totality to one another and are meaningful in that system (see Chapter 4).
3. Triangulation is the application of geometrical principles and axioms to determine distances between objects or places (if one side and two angles of a triangle are known, then the length of the other sides can be calculated from this information. This was the only feasible way of measuring distances over water and other obstacles (Oliver, 2005: 11).

4. By the end of the war in 1815, all areas south of Birmingham had been mapped, mostly at the two-inch (1: 31,680) scale, with some maps published by the OS.

5. Full cost recovery was achieved through the formation of the National Interest Mapping Service Agreement, or NIMSA, and by 2006 the OS was achieving a balanced budget without NIMSA, and was finally self-funding. In 2007–2008 turnover was £118.3 million, with an operating profit recorded at £22.5 million (Oliver, 2005: 20).

6. This system was finally retired in 1996 after more than 33 years of service. It was based on research from observations of the first man-made satellite, the Soviet Sputnik, launched in 1957.

7. The final and 24th satellite was launched on 26 June 1993, completing the NAVSTAR system, since which the NAVSTAR system has simply been known as GPS (Nelson, 1999). The master control station for GPS is located at the Schriever Air Force Base in Colorado, which maintains the satellites and performs station-keeping and altitude controls on the satellites. System time is measured and managed by the US Naval Observatory in Washington DC (Goebel, 2002).

8. The US military did not make an accurate GPS signal available for commercial and civilian use until 2000, following the 1996 Presidential Decision Directive to review selective availability in 2000.

9. Foursquare make this database of places freely available to programmers and application developers through the Foursquare API.

10. Initially, Google maps were used for this, but in February 2012 Foursquare moved to the Openstreetmap standard. Both Openstreetmap and Google maps are indicative of the tile-based mapping technique that allows mapping applications to remain responsive while storing data through creating maps from a number of smaller tiled images (Sample and Ioup, 2010: 2).

11. Schonfeld (2010) has called for an end to the duplicate nature of this database creation, and for an open database of places, which will still be open to addition and comment from users but that will be more thorough and complete than the current competing databases. This database could self-correct over time, by rewarding good data over bad data through user feedback and could counter the possibility of geo-spam.

12. Fuchs (2008) positions this free labour in the context of a political economy of social networking, arguing that this kind of production is a transformation of everyday practices and entertainment choices into commodities to be sold for the commercial benefit of social networking companies.

13. This in itself is an example of a system being created by free labour or the audience commodity (Smythe, 2006).

3 The Phenomenology of Place

1. Transcendental subjectivity was criticised by Heidegger himself. In *Existence and Being* (1949) Heidegger characterises Being as fundamental ontology as ontology, and that ontology is something that blocks or obscures the truth of being-as-itself. Following this, Heidegger states "every philosophy which revolves around an indirect or direct conception of 'transcendence' remains

of necessity essentially an ontology, whether it achieves a new foundation of ontology or whether it assures us that it repudiates ontology as a conceptual freezing of experience" (Heidegger, 1998c: 289). As the positing of Dasein as an entity that discloses the world and understands it implies its nature as transcendental, Heidegger's criticism is explicitly of the concept of Dasein in as conceptualised in *Being and Time*.

2. The preface to *Being and Time* ends with these sentences: "To furnish a concrete elaboration of the question concerning the sense of 'Being' is the intention of the following treatise. The interpretation of Time as the horizon of every possible attempt to understand Being is its provisional goal" (Heidegger, 1962: 1).

3. When I am in an office I understand the principles and expectations of my actions in that setting, and how to utilise the myriad of objects in that environment such as the desks, computers and telephones to perform the tasks expected of an office worker. When there I do not consider the atomic, chemical or biological make up of those objects (unless I should consciously direct myself towards this task, which I am unqualified to do) but instead I interpret the meaning of these objects in the context in which I have found them, and act accordingly.

4. Even if I was to find myself in a situation alien to me – such as a war zone filled with ammunition and guns – I would still be striving to make sense of the situation; even if I did fail and my actions were inappropriate to the situation (as they no doubt would be).

5. Not only are the physical sciences criticised, but other views of analysing the world, such as Habermas' critical rationality (removal from the world) is also rendered impossible as it assumes beliefs seen objectively when in reality – according to the phenomenological view – there are only the practices and skills that are exhibited in the world (Dreyfus, 1990: 20).

6. A shop at the top of a hill may be geometrically closer than the supermarket store in the town, but because of the difficulty in getting there and my frequenting of the supermarket over time, it is not experientially closer.

7. This explanation can also explain how we can be experts in that which we have not experienced; a historian may not have experienced the English civil war, but through exposure to literature and sources of information, the existential locale of the English civil war is familiar to that historian (or near, rather than far). Jerkins (2009) makes the same point about the phenomenological nearness of Mars due to the cultural and scientific information on the Red Planet, and the relative distance of spaces on our own planet (e.g. the floor of the middle of the Atlantic Ocean) due to the lack of information available on those spaces.

8. In the semantically meaningful world, the other entities that reside there are not revealed to us in their entirety, but are instead either revealed as present-at-hand objects or ready-to-hand tools. If I was Huxley's (2007) noble savage from *Brave New World*, posited into the office environment of the early 21st century, then the objects I would encounter within that environment would not be of much use to me. They would be present-at-hand objects. That is not to say that they would not excite my curiosity; the noble savage might try to theorise as to what these objects are and what their uses might be from his perspective. However, the person that is accustomed to this

world would encounter these objects as ready-to-hand tools (Zeug in *Being and Time*, 1963: 97). That is, things to be used in a manner appropriate for that environment in accordance with customs and appropriateness for that situation.

9. This understanding of a free relationship with technology is dependent upon this freedom and realising of possibilities.

10. The mode of being is also known as the Mood of Dasein's being-in-the-world.

11. Although this may play a role in the manner of my handling of the wood, it is not the thing that creates the skilful handling of the wood characteristic of the carpenter.

12. The idea of world provided here is hermeneutically circular, as the character of the world (and therefore understanding of place) can only be revealed through taking things into care, but that this taking into care is also dependent upon an understanding of the role of the thing in that space that allows for the worlding of the world to be revealed through the use of things.

13. Malpas (2008: 99) notes that *Befindichkeit* has been translated as "state of mind" by Macquarrie and Robinson (1962) and as attunement by Stambaugh. Although I use attunement here, state of mind is equally good for explaining the towards-which that Dasein has to things in the world. State of mind may be more problematic as it may imply a choice in Dasein's being-towards, whereas this is not what Heidegger meant; *Befindlichkeit* is not chosen but is how Dasein is towards things at that time.

14. Jacobson (2006: 95) uses the example of a study in the home to illustrate this: at one time, the study is a place of accomplishment, at another a place of demands, tedium and anxiety. The mood of Dasein shapes the character of the place, and even when the same equipment is in that space the sense of place changes with the mood of Dasein. This is due to Dasein being responsible in disclosing the world, but also illustrates that world disclosure is dependent upon mood. The character of the world and place is a function of mood.

15. The concept of authenticity is linked to Heidegger's notion of "ownness" and ownership, in that Dasein's existence is its own existence. Dasein cannot be that of another, or cannot be explained and dwelled upon by another in the same way that Dasein can explain it itself. Dasein "has the structure of 'mineness'" (Heidegger, 1962: 67), and this is not something that occurs as an event but which is revealed to Dasein through living. This is not a wonderful explanation, but Heidegger himself notes that this is a phenomenon that is difficult to relay effectively. It is Dasein's "mineness" that is capable of being either authentic or inauthentic: "As modes of being, authenticity and inauthenticity ... are both grounded in the fact that any Dasein whatsoever is characterised by mineness" (Heidegger, 1962: 43). Moran (2000: 240) explains this passage as referring to authenticity and inauthenticity being modes of Dasein's being-in, as Dasein is always mine or yours, always individualised into the life of the individual. When we explain and relate to our own existence, we do so in either an authentic or inauthentic manner, or in some undifferentiated state between the two (Heidegger, 1962: 53). When I am experiencing an authentic mood, I am at "home with myself" in a deep, concrete experience of my "mineness". I can recognise possibilities and experiences as my own. Most of the time, Heidegger believes that we

do not live in this way, but instead experience the world in an indifferent manner or even in an inauthentic manner.

16. Heidegger's approach is therefore still phenomenological, although it is not concerned with the method of phenomenology in the later works, but instead with what there is in the world that affects Dasein's relationship to being itself.

17. Heidegger's aim is to uncover this more fundamental insight into how technology affects the relationship between being and understanding being. Humans can control technology, but even this control is informed by our "instrumental conception" (Heidegger, 1977: 5) of what technology is.

18. There is an anticipated objection to Heidegger's view of technology as a revealing (Heidegger, 1977: 12–13). Heidegger questions the validity of considering the Greek meaning of words when the fundamental question he is approaching is about modern technology. The discussion of ancient Greece and the chalice might appear redundant in the modern technological age of social networking and cyberspace. However, to assume that modern technology is based on modern science such as physics is to miss the point of Heidegger's argument. The development of science has depended upon the development of the technology that supports its empirical methodologies. As this is the case, science cannot be separated from technology; it cannot be the cause of technology as it is a part of the technology itself. What differences there are do not come from the technology itself, but from the orientation of modern technology to the world, and that modern technology's mode of revealing is not *poesis*, but a challenging that puts to nature an unreasonable demand that it supplies energy which cannot be replenished, but extracted and stored as such.

19. A phenomenon observable in western intensive farming practices and the collectivisation of agriculture in the former USSR (Gray, 2007: 138–139).

20. Modern technology may do for human relationships what agricultural mechanisation has done for farmland. The argument would be that as human interactions are mediated through computational devices (modern technology), their purpose is to extract as much information from as little communication as possible. Hence, instead of care and consideration being the key parts of interpersonal friendship communications, the communication which is technologically mediated is for the main part characterised by short, abbreviated communications with the aim of advancing as much information a possible with the least amount of energy or resource spent; the maximum gain for the minimum effort. Modern technology places users into the open; users are grasped in a manner which "unlocks" them and their potential as resources and which then allows other users to exploit them as resource, and the user to view other users in the same manner (Harman, 2007: 135).

21. The term poetic is used in difference to technological, and is not to be read as a synonym for poetry. The revealing could be termed *computational*, but this is closely associated with technological and so could easily be confused or misread. Poetic is used to both ascribe the revealing of place as different to technological while acknowledging the role of computational technology in the revealing of place being argued for in this and following chapters.

22. In the "Letter on Humanism," published in 1947 (2008), Heidegger stressed that the publication of the third division of *Being and Time* would have been called "Time and Being" and this would have entailed a reversal of the kind that the turn eventually became. However, given the language of metaphysics in the initial project, this project was not possible, as the thinking of *Being and Time* did not allow for the expression of the ideas in a clear manner; an annihilation of thought by metaphysics (Malpas, 2008: 151).

23. It could be argued that the problem of transcendence is something that obscures the question of being itself, in the same way that metaphysics is characterised as doing so in Heidegger's history of being.

24. The idea of *Ereignis* is complex in the sense that a translation into English is not direct, and even from the original German the term as used by Heidegger connotes many different elements (Malpas, 2008: 216). *Ereignis* has its roots in *"eräugnen"* (Malpas, 2008: 215), meaning to see or be evident, and this sense of the word is retained in this analysis. Most commonly, *Ereignis* is translated as "event," and in such an event I want to retain the idea of something being made visible through the occurrence of an event. Maly and Emad (1999) translate the word as "enowning" or that in connection with things that arise and appear and that they arise "into their own." Dreyfus (2004) defines *Ereignis* as "things coming into themselves by belonging together" and this, too, is an important interpretation, as it emphasises that the event involves things that become meaningful for Dasein in the everyday situation of being-with other things in a place or situation. This recalls clearly the idea of the referential totality that is the world from Chapter 5, and the idea of world as related to event is critical in understanding the significance of *Ereignis* in both Heidegger's philosophy and this thesis.

25. The idea of the hermeneutic circle of meaning is referred to in both *Being and Time* and "The Origin of the Work of Art" (2008).

26. The type of thinking here is important to define; for McHugh (2007), there is dialectic between meditative and poetic thinking. Meditative thinking refers to the kind of thinking that relies upon representation (and is therefore indicative of the technological mode of revealing) whereas poetic thinking is intuitive, and brings mystery to presence, that is the mystery of being; the question for Dasein (Young, 2002).

4 The Mobile Device as a Thing: The Gathering of Place Digitally

1. Harman (2002: 190) makes much of the unfavourable reception that Heidegger's concept of the fourfold has received from not only critics of his philosophy, but also commentators that are favourably disposed. As a result, many commentaries on Heidegger's philosophy ignore the concept altogether, and other critics are dismissive of the concept as pious gibberish (Harman, 2002: 190). This may be for a number of reasons: the particularly poetic character of both the writing and the sentiment of the fourfold, the seeming irrelevance of the discussion of multiple essences from a philosopher synonymous with technological essentialism, or just the sheer oddness of the idea itself.

2. I will from this point on use "divinities" in place of "Gods."

3. This is something Harman, in light of his idea of tool-being (2002), may disagree with, in that objects themselves could be accorded the status of disclosing entities, given that objects stand in relation to one another in their tool-being.

4. Heidegger explains the manner of dwelling in "Building, Thinking, Dwelling" (2008: 247) in that by dwelling: we save the earth by not exploiting it, not mastering it and not subjugating it. We receive the sky in allowing things to happen and unfold naturally. We await the divinities by opening ourselves to the divine (the sanctity of life, the special essence of the moment and so on). We accompany the mortals through attending to being-with and attuning our actions to this mode of being, rather than seeking instant gratification through using things.

5. Turkle (2007: 20) uses the term "thing" to describe evocative computational objects that bring together thoughts and feelings (in the use of the device for communicative purposes) and feeling at one with the object or intimate with the thing. While I retain the Heideggerian use and sense of the term, it is interesting to note how the definition is used by others when discussing ostensibly the same devices.

6. Admittedly, Harman's account of tool-being (2002) offers some affordability to such an account, but the positing of phenomenological properties to non-humans is problematic in the sense of how one would ever be able to verify such an idea – Berry (2012) calls this the "anti-correlationist paradox." The speculative realism movement that has emerged through the work of Harman and others takes this idea of the relations between non-human actors as akin to the relation between Dasein and things as a possible phenomenological system, but for the purposes of this thesis such a view is unnecessary and problematic with regard to the role of the human in worlding.

7. It should be noted that if one tries to check-in to a venue too far away from that venue on Foursquare, the application states that you are too far away based on the location data provided by a-GPS.

8. Although only three satellites are needed for triangulation, the system uses more to correct any time errors that may occur in the lag between device and satellite.

9. This information can be shared with other social networking tools, like Twitter and Facebook. In this check-in, that sharing facility has not been used.

5 Sharing Location with Locative Social Media

1. Boellstorff (2008: 53) notes that the first recognisable ethnographies of virtual worlds were conducted by Michael Rosenberg in 1992 (ethnography of WolfMOO), and by John Masterton in 1994, who conducted an ethnography of Ancient Anguish. These ethnographies were of text-based virtual worlds, and many other ethnographies of such environments have been conducted since those early studies, focussing on specific topics of interest within such environments. These include studies on community (Baym, 2000; Blascovich, 2002; Hudson-Smith, 2002), identity (Bromberg, 1996; Donath, 1999; Rheingold,

2000) and of multiple virtual worlds (Fornäs et al., 2002; Juul, 2005). While these works provide examples of virtual ethnography, they also show considerable differences between one another in the approach taken to ethnography and the nature and analysis of the data collected.

2. http://www.surveymonkey.com/s/XCCH922.
3. Superuser status is conferred on users who check in frequently or enter new venue information into Foursquare.
4. There are measures one can take to maintain a high level of privacy when using LBSN. Foursquare offers the option to check-in "off the grid," which means that the check-in is not shared across the social network, and sharing with other social networks is optional. However, "off the grid" check-ins do not generate points for the Foursquare "game" and do not contribute to mayorships or the accrual of badges. The data from the "off the grid" check-in is still of course compiled and stored by Foursquare.
5. Or as Latour (2007: 245) would argue, *plasma* – those actors that are outside a network and therefore not visible when part of or considering the network.
6. As a tool in the world that shapes understanding of the world, the device is withdrawn but in order to operate it can never be fully withdrawn; this is what Harman refers to when ascribing "subterranean depths" to entities in the world (Harman 2009: 193). There are levels that cannot be in the conscious experience of Dasein as it encounters things in the world. This apparent paradox points to a computational understanding of the world being shaped by the device that is withdrawn from conscious experience but necessarily not fully withdrawn, as it continues to shape experience through the provision of data, but in a manner that is unobtrusive as the device remains ready-to-hand. The continual withdrawal of the device is useful in thinking about the status of the device as a thing, in that its "thinging" is always a present possibility given its functioning and operation.

6   The Social Capital of Locative Social Media

1. By behaviourally, I am not referring to the philosophical position of behaviourism where mental states are inferred (or explained away) by the observed actions of the person, but instead to the practices of use of LBSN in everyday life as an indication of the phenomenological revealing of place when using LBSN.
2. Latour's (2007: 266) concept of plasma (that which falls outside a network) is useful here in that Foursquare has failed in forming an alliance with the user and so falls away from usage, as it is not seen as a useful actor in the everyday functioning of this user.
3. See Michael and Michael (2009); Friedland and Sommer (2010); Mascetti et al. (2010); Ozer et al. (2010) amongst others.

7   Conclusions

1. It is of course worth noting that the particular tool or device focused upon in this book is a device with a haptic interface, and as such its use is always close to the user in any given environment. This proximity is not the only factor

in the revealing of place, however, as, if it were, then LBSN on smartphones would always reveal place; the towards-which or intention of use is therefore vital to the possibility of revealing of place.

2. In Heidegger's own terms, man always dwells poetically (Heidegger, 1971: 209–227).

3. Heidegger's first law of phenomenology is that what is obvious escapes our notice (Heidegger, 1992: 135). The contention is that metaphysics provides a necessary appearance of ground for each epoch of intelligibility. This contention must be understood in the context of Nietzsche's project of showing metaphysics as a series of untruths, by dislodging the ontological anchoring of metaphysical theories (Nietzsche, 2003: 10; Thomson, 2005: 20). Indeed, Nietzsche's groundless metaphysics implodes the metaphysical tradition, with the will-to-power offering no ground at all, only an endless repetition of the will acting in its own interests. The legacy of this metaphysical theory is the cybernetic epoch of enframing, as the "will to will" leads to a following of what can be used through desires, reducing all things to resources. Heidegger would argue that all metaphysics are like this, in that they "think" this way and that the metaphysical grounding is inexhaustible, in that it can interpret the world in any way. Hence, Kant's metaphysics and Nietzsche's metaphysics, while explaining what-is differently, are a product of the same mode of thinking, and neither is sufficient to explain the world as it is, but both metaphysical projects of grounding have an onto-theological structure (Thomson, 2005: 30).

4. Bishop (2010) uses this concept of metaphysics as ontotheology as a means to show that transhumanist philosophers deploy ontologies of power and a theology that allows their metaphysics to beget its own politics and ethics.

5. Such technological dependence or integration has been argued to be problematic in the context of cognition and skills (Carr, 2011), while others (Shirkey, 2010) see such an integration as beneficial, and so in itself is a topic in the humanities that is provoking some debate.

6. The augmented reality browser "Layar" could be an appropriate example of the kind of service proposed.

7. Arguably, the gamification model, with the eye-catching increases in user numbers that may be attributed to the novelty of the game model during 2010 and 2011, was a major factor in attracting large capital investment in the company, including a $50 million investment in June 2011 that valued the company at the time at $600 million, on the basis of the high value of the then ten million users (Lacy, 2011).

Bibliography

Adams, C. (2010).Teachers building, dwelling, thinking with slideware. *The Indo-Pacific Journal of Phenomenology*, 10 (2), pp. 1–12.

Arthur, C. (2010). Ordnance Survey launches free downloadable maps. *The Guardian*, April 01, 2010. http://www.guardian.co.uk/technology/2010/apr/01/ordnance-survey-maps-download-free. Retrieved 01/06/2010.

Atkinson, P. and Hammersley, M. (1989). *Ethnography: Principles in Practice.* New York: Routledge.

Barreneche, C. (2012). Governing the geocoded world: Environmentality and the politics of location platforms. *Convergence*, 18 (r3), pp. 331–351.

Bassett, C. (2012), Canonicalism and the computational turn. In D. M. Berry (Ed.), *Understanding Digital Humanities* (pp. 105–126). London: Palgrave Macmillan.

Batty, M. (1997). Virtual geography. *Futures*, 29 (4), pp. 337–352.

Batty, M. (1997b). The computable city. *International Planning Studies*, 2 (2), pp. 155–173.

Berry, D. M. (2004). Internet research: Privacy, ethics and alienation – An open source approach. *The Journal of Internet Research*, 14 (4), pp. 323–332.

Berry, D. M. (2008). *Copy, Rip, Burn: The Politics of Copyleft and Open Source.* London: Pluto Press.

Berry, D. M. (2011). *The Philosophy of Software: Code and Mediation in the Digital Age.* London: Palgrave/Macmillan.

Berry, D. M. (2012). The new bifurcation? Object-oriented ontology and computation, *Stunlaw*, http://stunlaw.blogspot.com/2012/06/new-bifurcation-object-oriented.html. Retrieved June 11, 2012.

Berry, D. M. (2012b). Glitch ontology, *Stunlaw*, http://stunlaw.blogspot.no/2012/05/glitch-ontology.html. Retrieved June 11, 2012.

Berry, D. M. (2012c). Life in code and software: Mediated life in a complex computational ecology, *Open Humanities Press*, http://www.livingbooksaboutlife.org/books/Life_in_Code_and_Software. Retrieved June 11, 2012.

Bilandzic, M. and Foth, M. (2012). A review of locative media, mobile and embodied spatial interaction. *International Journal of Human-Computer Studies*, 70 (1), pp. 66–71.

Bishop, J. P. (2010). Transhumanism, metaphysics and the posthuman God. *Journal of Medicine and Philosophy*, 35, pp. 700–720.

Blattner, W. (2007). *Heidegger's Being and Time: A Reader's Guide (Reader's Guides).* New York: Continuum International Publishing Group.

Boellstorff, T., Nardi, B., Pearce, C., & Taylor, T. L. (2012). *Ethnography and virtual worlds: A handbook of method.* Princeton University Press. Boellstorff (2008) is in the notes for this section, reference for bibliography: Boellstorff, T. (2008). *Coming of Age in Second Life: An Anthropologist Explores the Virtually Human.* Princeton: Princeton University Press.

Bogost, I. (2011). *Gamification is Bullshit.* http://www.bogost.com/blog/gamification_is_bullshit.shtml. Retrieved September 07, 2011.

Bogost, I. (2012). *Alien Phenomenology, or What its Like to be a Thing (Posthumanities)*. Minneapolis: University of Minnesota Press.

Borges, J. L. and Hurley, A. (1998). *Collected Fictions*. New York: Viking.

Bourdieu, P. (1972). *Outline of a Theory of Practice*. Cambridge: Cambridge University.

Bourdieu, P. (1985). The forms of capital. In *Handbook of Theory and Research for the Sociology of Education*, (Ed.) J. G. Richardson. New York: Greenwood, pp. 241–258.

Boyd, D. (2014). *It's Complicated: The Social Lives of Networked Teens*. New Haven: Yale University Press.

Brassier, R. (2007). *Nihil Unbound: Enlightenment and Extinction*. London: Palgrave/Macmillan.

Bull, M. (2000). *Sounding Out the City: Personal Stereos and the Management of Everyday Life*. London: Berg.

Burke, M., Kraut, R., and Marlow, C. (2011). *Social Capital on Facebook: Differentiating Uses and Users*. ACM CHI 2011: Conference on Human Factors in Computing Systems.

Burke, M., Marlow, C., and Lento, T. (2010). *Social Network Activity and Social Well-Being*. ACM CHI 2010: Conference on Human Factors in Computing Systems, 1909–1912.

Butcher, M. (2012). Welcome to Apple's iOS6 map – where Berlin is now called "Schoneiche". *Techcrunch*. http://techcrunch.com/2012/09/20/welcome-to-apples-ios6-map-where-berlin-is-now-called-schoeneiche/ retrieved 11/1/2013.

Campbell, S. and Kwak, N. (2011). Mobile communication and civil society: Linking patterns and places of use to engagement with others in public. *Human Communication Research*, 37, pp. 207–222.

Campbell, S. and Kwak, N. (2012). Mobile communication and strong network ties: Shrinking or expanding spheres of public discourse? *New Media and Society*, 14, pp. 262–280.

Campbell, S. W. and Ling, R. S. (2008). Effects of mobile communication. In J. Bryant and M. Oliver (Eds.), *Media Effects: Advances in Theory and Research* (3rd ed., pp. 592–606). Mahwah, NJ: Lawrence Erlbaum Associates.

Carnap, R. (1995). *Introduction to the Philosophy of Science*. New York: Dover.

Carr, N. (2011). *The Shallows: What the Internet is Doing to our Brains*. London: W.W. Norton and Co.

Chalmers, D. J. (1994). On implementing a computation. *Minds and Machines*, 4, pp. 391–402.

Chun, W. H. (2011). *Programmed Visions: Software and Memory*. Cambridge, Mass.: MIT Press.

Concannon, K. (1998). The contemporary space of the border: Gloria Anzaldua's Borderlands and William Gibson's Neuromancer. *Textual Practice*, 12 (3), pp. 429–442.

Copeland, B. J. (1996). What is computation? *Syntheses*, 108, pp. 335–359.

Coyne, R. (1995). *Designing information technology in the postmodern age: From method to metaphor*. Cambridge MA: MIT Press.

Coyne, R. (2010). *The Tuning of Place: Social Spaces and Pervasive Digital Media*. London: MIT Press.

Crampton, J. (2009). *Mapping Without a Net: The Politics, Sovereignty and Ontology of Cartography*. Proceedings of the 24th international Cartographic

162 *Bibliography*

Conference. icaci.org/documents/ICC_proceedings/ICC2009/html/nonref/27_6. pdf. Retrieved June 01, 2010.

Crandall, J. (2011). An actor of the street: Events, agencies and gatherings. *SubStance*, 126: 40 (3), pp. 49–66.

Crawford, A. and Goggin, G. (2009). Geomobile web: Locative. Technologies and mobile media. *Australian Journal of Communication*, 36 (1), pp. 97–109

De Notaris, D. (2010). *Social Network Sites and Life – Sharing*. 3rd ESA Sociology of Culture RN mid-term Conference: Culture and the Making of Worlds.

De Souza e Silva, A. and Frith, J. (2010). Locational privacy in public spaces: Media discourses on location-aware mobile technologies. *Communication, Culture & Critique*, 3 (4), pp. 503–525.

Deleuze, G. and Guattari, F. (1972). *Anti-Oedipus (Translated by Hurley, R., Seem, M. and Lane, H.R.)*. London: Continuum.

Descartes, R. (1997). *Key Philosophical Writings*. London: Wordsworth Classics.

Descartes, R. (2001). *Discourse on Method, Optics, Geometry and Meteorology*. Indianapolis: Hackett.

Dodge, M. and Kitchin, R. (2004). *Code, Space and Everyday Life*, Casa Working Paper Series, http://www.casa.ucl.ac.uk/working_papers/paper81.pdf. Retrieved June 11, 2012.

Dodge, M. and Kitchin, R. (2011). *Code/Space: Software and Everyday Life*. Cambridge MA: MIT Press.

Dourish, P. (2001). *Where the Action Is: The Foundations of Embodied Interaction*. Cambridge: MIT Press.

Dreyfus, H. L. (1989). On the ordering of things: Being and power in Heidegger and Foucault. *The Southern Journal of Philosophy*, 28 (1), pp. 83–96.

Dreyfus, H. L. (1990). *Being-in-the-World: A Commentary on Heidegger's Being and Time, Division I*. London: The MIT Press.

Dreyfus, H. L. (1993). Heidegger on the connection between nihilism, art, technology, and politics. In Charles Guignon (Ed), *The Cambridge Companion to Heidegger* (pp. 289–316). Cambridge: Cambridge University Press.

Dreyfus, H. L. (2004) *Being and Power: Heidegger and Foucault*. http://socrates. berkeley.edu/~hdreyfus/html/paper_being.html. Retrieved April 03, 2006.

Dreyfus, H. and Spinoza, C. (1997). *Highway Bridges and Feasts: Heidegger and Borgmann on How to Affirm Technology*. http://www.focusing.org/apm_papers/ dreyfus.html. Retrieved May 03, 2006.

Dreyfus, H. L. and Wrathall, M. (2009). *A Companion to Phenomenology and Existentialism*. London: Blackwell.

Elden, S. (2002) *Mapping the Present: Heidegger, Foucault and the Project of a Spatial History*. London: Continuum.

Elden, S. (2012). Worlds, temperaments, engagements: Introducing Peter Sloterdijk. In Stuart Elden (Ed.), *Sloterdijk Now* (pp. 1–16). Cambridge: Polity.

Elden, S. and Mendieta, E. (2009). Being-with as making worlds: The "second coming" of Peter Sloterdijk. *Environment and Planning D: Society and Space*, 27 (1), pp. 1–11.

Ellison, N. B., Steinfield, C., and Lampe, C. (2011). Connection strategies: Social capital implications of Facebook-enabled communication practices. *New Media & Society*, 13 (6), pp. 873–892.

Ellison, N. B., Lampe, C., Steinfeld, C., and Vitak, J. (2011). With a little help from my friends: How social network sites affect social capital processes. In Z.

Papacharissi (Ed.), *A Networked Self: Identity, Community and Culture on Social Network Sites* (pp. 124–145). London: Routledge.

Elmer, G. (2010). *Locating Migrating Media*. New York: Lexington Books.

Evans, L. (2011a). *Object Oriented Philosophy – The nature of relations between humans and computational objects*. Proceedings of the AISB '11. http://www.aisb.org.uk/convention/aisb11/. Retrieved May 01, 2011.

Evans, L. (2011b). Location-based services: Transformation of the experience of space. *Journal of Location Based Services*, 5 (3–4), pp. 242–260.

Evans, L. (2013). How to build a map for free: Immaterial labour and location-based social networking. In G. Lovink and M. Rasch (Eds.), *Unlike Us: Social Media Monopolies and Their Alternatives*. Amsterdam: Institute for Network Cultures.

Evans, L. (2014). Being-towards the social: Mood and orientation to location-based social media, computational things and applications. *New Media and Society*, doi: 10.1177/1461444813518183

Fairclough, N. and Wodak, R. (1997). Critical discourse analysis. In T. A.Van Dijk (Ed.), *Discourse as Social Interaction* (pp. 258–284). London: Sage.

Fairclough, N. (1989). *Language and Power*. London: Longman.

Fairclough, N. (1992). *Discourse and Social Change*. Cambridge, MA: Wiley-Blackwell.

Fairclough, N. (1995) *Critical Discourse Analysis: The Critical Study of Language*. Harlow: Longman

Farman, J. (2012). *Mobile Interface Theory: Embodied Space and Locative Media*. Routledge: New York.

Feenberg, A. (1999). *Questioning Technology*. London: Routledge.

Feenberg, A. (2003). Modernity theory and technological studies: Reflections on bridging the gap. In T. Misa, P. Brey and A. Feenberg (Eds.), *Modernity and Technology*. Cambridge, MA: MIT press.

Flyvbjerg, B. (2006). Five misunderstandings about case study research. *Qualitative Enquiry*, 12 (2), pp. 219–246.

Fodor, J. A. (1981). The mind-body problem. *Scientific American*, 244, pp. 114–123.

Foucault, M. (1982). *The Archaeology of Knowledge & The Discourse on Language*. New York: Pantheon.

Foucault, M. (1994). *The Order of Things: An Archaeology of Human Sciences*. New York: Vintage.

Foucault, M. (1995). *Discipline & Punish: The Birth of the Prison*. New York: Vintage.

Foucault, M. (1998). *The History of Sexuality Volume 1: The Will to Knowledge*. London: Penguin.

Foursquare (2011). *How Do I Get The Overshare Badge?* http://www.4squarebadges.com/foursquare-badge-list/overshare-badge/. Retrieved July 17, 2011.

Foursquare (2011b). *1UP: The Importance of Platforms and How We're Extending Ours*. http://blog.foursquare.com/2011/03/14/1up-the-importance-of-platforms-and-how-we%E2%80%99re-extending-ours/. Retrieved April 04, 2011.x

Foursquare (2011c). *Wow! The Foursquare Community has Over 10,000,000 Members!* http://blog.foursquare.com/2011/06/20/holysmokes10millionpeople/. Retrieved August 01, 2011.

Foursquare (2011d). *Thanks for a Great Year!* http://blog.foursquare.com/2011/12/23/thanks-for-a-great-year-happy-holidays-and-we-look-forward-to-building-more-awesome-things-for-you-in-2012/. Retrieved January 03, 2012.

Foursquare (2012). *Anywhere in the World, Foursquare Explore can Find you Something Interesting.* http://blog.foursquare.com/2012/01/12/anywhere-in-the-world-foursquare-explore-can-find-you-something-interesting-now-on-your-computer/. Retrieved January 15, 2012.

Foursquare (2014). *Thanks for Being with Us for Five Years. A Brand New Foursquare is Almost Ready for You.* Email communication: received July 23, 2014.

Fresco, N. (2010). Explaining computation without semantics: Keeping it simple. *Journal for Artificial Intelligence, Philosophy and Cognitive Science*, 20 (2), pp. 165–183.

Friedland, G. and Sommer, R. (2010). *Cybercasing the joint: On the privacy implications of geotagging.* In Proceedings of Fifth USENIX Workshop on Hot Topics in Security (HotSec10).

Frith, J. (2012). Splintered space: Hybrid spaces and differential mobility. *Mobilities*, 7 (1), pp. 131–149.

Fuchs, C. (2008). A Contribution to the critique of the political economy of the internet. *European Journal of Communication*, 24 (1), pp. 69–87.

Fuller, M. (2003). *Behind the Blip: Essays on the Culture of Software.* New York: Autonomedia.

Fuller, M. (2008). *Software Studies: A Lexicon.* MIT Press: Cambridge, MA

Galloway, A. R. (2004). *Protocol: How Control Exists After Decentralization.* MIT Press: Cambridge, MA

Gazzard, A. (2011). Location, location, location: Collecting space and place in mobile media. *Convergence*, 17 (4), pp. 405–417.

Geertz, C. (1973). *The Interpretation of Cultures: Selected Essays by Clifford Geertz.* New York: Basic Books.

Gershenfeld, N. (1999). *When Things Start to Think.* New York: Henry Holt.

Gibson, W. (1984). *Neuromancer.* New York: Ace Books.

Gibson, W. (1995). *Burning Chrome and Other Stories* (Paperback ed.). Hammersmith, London: HarperCollins.

Gibson, W. (1999). *The Science in Science Fiction: NPR Talk of the Nation (audio recording).* November 30th, 1999, http://www.npr.org/templates/story/story.php?storyId=1067220 Listened October 30, 2011.

Goebel, G. (2002). *Navigation Satellites and GPS.* www.faqs.org/docs/air.ttgps.html. Retrieved April 02, 2009.

Goffman, E. (1959). *The Presentation of Self in Everyday Life.* London: Penguin.

Goggin, G. (2009). Adapting the mobile phone: The iPhone and its consumption. *Continuum*, 23 (2), pp. 231–244.

Gordon, E. (2008). Towards a theory of networked locality. *First Monday*, 13 (10), 6/10/2008. http://www.firstmonday.org/htbin/cgiwrap/bin/ojs/index.php/fm/article/view/2157/2035. Retrieved 01/07/2012.

Gordon, E. and de Souza e Silva, A. (2011). *Net Locality: Why Location Matters in a Networked World.* Chichester: Wiley-Blackwell.

Gordon, E., Baldwin-Philippi, J., and Balestra, M. (2013). Why we engage: How theories of human behavior contribute to our understanding of civic engagement in a digital era. *Berkman Center Research Publication*, 21, pp. 1–29.

Gorner, P. (2006). *Heidegger, Phenomenology and the Essence of Technology*, www.abdn.ac.uk/philosophy/endsandmeans/vol2no1/gorner.shtml. Retrieved July 21, 2007.

Grant, I. H. (2006). *Philosophies of Nature after Schelling.* London and New York: Continuum.

Gray, J. (2002). *Straw Dogs: Thoughts on Humans and Other Animals.* London: Granta.

Greenfield, A. (2006). *Everywhere: The Dawning Age of Ubiquitous Computing.* Berkley, CA: Peachpit Press.

Guignon, C. (2004). The history of being. In Hubert L. Dreyfus and Mark A. Wrathall (Ed.), *A Companion to Heidegger* (pp. 392–406). New York: Blackwell.

Gunkel, D. and Taylor, P. A. (2014). *Heidegger and the Media.* London: Polity.

Hair, N. and Clark, M. (2003). An enhanced virtual ethnography: The role of critical theory, refereed conference proceedings. *3rd International Critical Management Studies Conference Lancaster, United Kingdom.*

Hampton, K. N., Livio, O., and Goulet, L. S. (2010). The social life of wireless urban spaces: Internet use, social networks and the public realm. *Journal of Communication,* 60, pp. 701–720.

Harman, G. (2002). *Tool-Being: Heidegger and the Metaphysics of Objects.* London: Open Court.

Harman, G. (2005). *Guerrilla Metaphysics.* London: Open Court.

Harman, G. (2007). *Heidegger Explained: From Phenomenon to Thing (Ideas Explained).* London: Open Court.

Harman, G. (2009). *Prince of Networks: Bruno Latour and Metaphysics (Anamnesis).* Albany: Re.Press,

Hayles, N. K. (2009). RFID: Human agency and meaning in information-intensive environments. *Theory, Culture and Society,* 26 (2–3), pp. 47–72.

Hayles, N. K. (2005). *My Mother was a Computer: Digital Subjects and Literary Texts.* Chicago: University of Chicago Press.

Heidegger, M. (1947/1994). *Bremer und Freiburger Vortrage.* Frankfurt am Main: Klostermann.

Heidegger, M. (1949). *Existence and Being (1st American ed.).* Chicago: H. Regnery.

Heidegger, M. (1962). *Being and Time.* Oxford: Blackwell.

Heidegger, M. (1971). *Poetry, Language, Thought (trans. A. Hoffstadter).* New York: Harper and Row.

Heidegger, M. (1977). *The Question Concerning Technology, and Other Essays.* New York: Harper Perennial.

Heidegger, M. (1992). *History of the Concept of Time.* Indianapolis: Indiana University Press.

Heidegger, M. (1994). *Basic Questions of Philosophy: Selected "problems" of "logic"* (Trans. Rojcewicz, R. and Schuwer, A.). Indiana: Indiana University Press.

Heidegger, M. (1998). *Parmenides.* (Trans. Schuwer, A. and Rojcewicz, R.) Bloomington: Indiana University Press.

Heidegger, M. (1998b). Traditional language and technological language. *Journal of Philosophical Research,* 23, pp.129–145.

Heidegger, M. (1998c). *Pathmarks* (Ed. W. MacNeill). Cambridge: Cambridge University Press.

Heidegger, M. (1999). *Contributions to Philosophy (From Enowning).* Indiana: Indiana University Press.

Heidegger, M. (2002). *Off the Beaten Track* (Trans. J. Young and K. Haynes). Cambridge: Cambridge University Press.

Heidegger, M. (2007). *The Heidegger Reader* (edited with an introduction by Gunter Figal). Bloomington: Indiana University Press.

Heidegger, M. (2008). *Basic Writings: From Being and Time (1927) to The Task of Thinking (1964)* (Rev. and expanded ed.). London: Routledge.

Hine, C. M. (2000). *Virtual Ethnography.* Thousand Oaks, CA: Sage Publications Ltd.

Hjorth, L. (2009). The big bang: An example of mobile media as new media. *ACM Computers in Entertainment*, 7 (2), pp. 1–13.

Hjorth, L. (2011). Still Mobile: Networked Mobile Media, Video Content and Users in Seoul, in R. Somers Miles & G. Lovink (Eds.) *Video Vortex Reader II.* Amsterdam: Institute of Networked Cultures, pp. 195–210.

Hjorth, L. (2012). Still mobile: A case study on mobility, home and being away in Shanghai. *Mobile Technologies and Place*, (Eds.) G. Goggin & R. Wilken, New York: Routledge, pp. 140–156.

Hjorth, L. (2013). Relocating the mobile: A case study of locative media in Seoul, South Korea. *Convergence*, 19, pp. 237–249.

Hjorth, L., Wilken, R., and Gu, K. (2012). Ambient intimacy: A case study of the iPhone, presence and location-based social networking in Shanghai, China. In L. Hjorth, J. Burgess and I. Richardson (Eds.), *Studying Mobile Media: Cultural Technologies, Mobile Communication and the iPhone* (pp. 43–62). New York, NY: Routledge.

Honda Worldwide History (2009). http://world.honda.com/history/challenge/ 1981navigationsystem/index.html. Retrieved March 03, 2011.

Hubbard, P., Kitchen, R., Bartley, B., and Fuller, D. (2002). *Thinking Geographically: Space, Theory and Contemporary Human Geography.* London: Continuum Press.

Humphreys, L. (2005). Cellphones in Public: Social interactions in a wireless era. *New Media and Society*, 7 (6), pp. 801–833.

Humphreys, L. (2008). Mobile social networks and social practice: A case study of Dodgeball. *Journal of Computer-Mediated Communication*, 13 (2008), pp. 341–360.

Humphreys, L. (2010). Mobile social networks and urban public space. *New Media and Society*, 12 (5), pp. 763–778.

Humphreys, L. (2013). Mobile social media: Future challenges and opportunities. *Mobile Media and Communication*, 1, pp. 20–25.

Humphreys, L., Gill, P., and Krishnamurthy, B. (2010). *How much is too much? Privacy issues on Twitter.* Proceedings of the International Communication Association Conference, at http://www2.research.att.com/~bala/papers/ica10. pdf. Retrieved December 02, 2010.

Huxley, A. (2007). *Brave New World.* London: Vintage Classics.

Ihde, D. (1990). *Technology and the Lifeworld: From Garden to Earth.* Bloomington and Indianopolis: Indiana University Press.

IMS research (2011). *Global Smartphone Sales Will Top 420 Million Devices in 2011.* http://imsresearch.com/press-release/Global_Smartphones_Sales_Will_Top_420_ Million_Devices_in_2011_Taking_28_Percent_of_all_Handsets_According_to_ IMS_Research. Retrieved December 01, 2012.

Ingold, T. (2000). *The Perception of the Environment: Essays on Livelihood, Dwelling and Skill.* London, UK: Routledge.

Ingold, T. (2011). *Being Alive: Essays on Movement, Knowledge and Description.* London, UK: Routledge.

Inwood, M. (2002). *Heidegger: A very short introduction* (Very Short Introductions). New York: Oxford University Press, USA.

Jacobson, K. (2004). Agoraphobia and hypochondria as disorders of dwelling. *International Studies in Philosophy*, 36 (2), pp. 31–45.

Jacobson, K. (2006). *Being at Home: A Phenomenological Analysis of the Experience of Space*. Pennsylvania State University Doctoral Dissertation, 2007. http://gradworks.umi.com/32/48/3248351.html. Retrieved September 21, 2011.

Jacobson, K. (2009) A developed nature: A phenomenological account of the experience of home. *Continental Philosophy Review*, 42, pp. 355–373.

Jacobson, K. (2010). The experience of home and the space of citizenship. *The Southern Journal of Philosophy*, 48 (3), 219–245.

Jacobson, K. (2011). Embodied domestics, embodied politics: Women, home and agoraphobia. *Human Studies*, 34, pp. 1–21.

Jameson, F. (1991). *Postmodernism, or the Cultural Logic of Late Capitalism*. Durham: Duke University Press.

Jorgensen, M. and Philips, L. (2002). *Discourse Analysis as Theory and Method*. London: Sage.

Kaczynski, T. (2005). *The Unabomber Manifesto: Industrial Society and Its Future*. Minneapolis: Filiquarian Publishing.

Kammersell, W. and Dean, M. (2006). *Conceptual Search: Incorporating Geospatial Data into Semantic Queries*. In: Terra Cognita – Directions to the Geospatial Semantic Web, Athens, GA.

Kant, I. (1999). *Critique of Pure Reason (The Cambridge Edition Works of Immanuel Kant)*. Cambridge: Cambridge University Press.

Kelly, K. (2010). *What Technology Wants*. New York: Viking.

Kiss, J. (2010). Foursquare: One Million users and a deal immanent.... *The Guardian*, April 26, 2010. http://www.guardian.co.uk/media/pda/2010/apr/26/location-foursquare-acquisition. Retrieved May 24, 2010.

Kitchin, R. (1994), Cognitive maps: What are they and why study them? *Journal of Environmental Psychology*, 14, pp. 1–19.

Kitchin, R. and Kneale, J. (2005), *Lost in Space: Geographies of Science Fiction*, London: A&C Black.

Kitchin, R., Gleeson, J. and Dodge, M. (2012). Unfolding Mapping Practices: A New Epistemology for Cartography. *Transactions of the Institute of British Geographers*, 38 (3): 480–496.

Kittler, F. A. (1999). *Gramophone, Film, Typewriter*. Stamford: Stamford University Press.

Kloet, S. (2007). TomTom Holders Approve Takeover of TeleAtlas. *Wall Street Journal*, 4/12/2007. http://www.wsj.com/articles/SB119677803171513059 retrieved 14/10/2011.

Kockelmans, J. J. (1970). Heideggeron time and being. *The Southern Journal of Philosophy*, 8, pp. 319–340.

Korzybski, A. (1933). A non-aristotelian system and its necessity for rigour in mathematics and physics. *Science and Sanity*, 1933, pp. 747–761.

Kozinets, R. (2002). The field behind the screen: Using netnography for marketing research in online communities. *Journal of Marketing Research*, 39 (1), p. 61.

Kuhn, T. S. (1987). What are scientific revolutions? In L. Kruger, L. J. Daston and M. Heidelberger (Eds.), *The Probabilistic Revolution, Vol. 1: Ideas in History* (pp. 7–22). Cambridge, MA: MIT Press.

Lacy, S. (2011). *Foursquare Closes $50M at a $600M Valuation*. Techcrunch, June 24, 2011, http://techcrunch.com/2011/06/24/foursquare-closes-50m-at-a-600m-valuation/. Retrieved January 03, 2012.

Laermans, R. (2011). The attention regime: On mass media and the information society. In *Media Res:Peter Sloterdijk's Spherical Poetics of Being* (pp. 115–133). Amsterdam: Amsterdam University Press.

Latour, B (1987). *Science in Action: How to Follow Scientists and Engineers through Society*. Cambridge: Harvard University Press.

Latour, B. (2007). *We Have Never Been Modern*. Cambridge: Harvard University Press.

Latour, B., November, V., and Camacho-Hubner, E. (2010). Entering a risky territory: Space in the age of digital navigation. *Environment and Planning*, 28 (4), pp. 581–591.

Law, J. (2002). Objects and Spaces. *Theory, Culture and Society*, 19 (5/6), pp. 91–105.

Lefebvre, H. (1974). *The Production of Space*. Oxford: Blackwell.

Lessig, L. (1999). *Code and Other Laws of Cyberspace*. New York: Basic Books.

Ling, R. and Campbell, S. W. (Eds.) (2011). *Mobile communication: Bringing us together and tearing us apart*. New Brunswick, NJ: Transaction Publishers.

Ling, R. and Horst, H. A. (2011). Mobile communication in the global south. *New Media & Society*, 13 (3), pp. 363–374.

Lozar, J. M. (2008). Nietzsche and Heidegger. *Synthesis Philosophica*, 45 (1), pp. 121–133.

Lynch, K. (1960). *The Image of the City*. Cambridge, Massachusetts: MIT Press.

Maanen, J. V. (1988). *Tales of the Field: On Writing Ethnography (Chicago Guides to Writing, Editing, and Publishing)*. Chicago: University Of Chicago Press.

Mackenzie, A. (2003). *Transduction: Invention, Innovation and Collective Life*. www.lancs.ac.uk/staff/mackenza/papers/transduction.pdf. Retrieved March 29, 2012.

Mackenzie, A. (2006). *Cutting Code: Software and Sociality*. New York: Peter Lang.

Mackenzie, A. (2010). *Wirelessness: Radical Empiricism in Networked Cultures*. Cambridge, Mass.: MIT Press.

Madden, M., Lenhart, A., Duggan, M., Cortesi, S., and Glasser, U. (2013). Teens and Technology 2013. Pew Research Center and The Berkman Center for Internet and Society. Retrieved from http://www.pewinternet.org/Reports/2013/Teens-and-Tech.aspx

Magellan GPS. (2009). *Magellan GPS – Sitemap*. http://corp.magellangps.com/en/aboutUs. Retrieved June 02, 2010

Malpas, J. E. (2000). Uncovering the space of disclosedness: Heidegger, technology and the problem of spatiality in *being and time*. In H. L. Dreyfus, M. A. Wrathall and J. E. Malpas (Eds.), *Heidegger, Authenticity, and Modernity: Essays in Honor of Hubert L. Dreyfus*(pp. 205–227). Cambridge, Mass.: MIT Press.

Malpas, J. E. (2008). *Heidegger's Topology: Being, Place, World*. Cambridge: MIT Press.

Mann, C. and Stewart, F. (2000). *Internet Communication and Qualitative Research: A Handbook for Researching Online (New Technologies for Social Research series)*. Thousand Oaks, CA: Sage Publications Ltd.

Mann, S., Nolan, J., and Wellman, B. (2002). Sousveillance: Inventing and using wearable computing devices for data collection in surveillance environments. *Surveillance & Society*, 1 (3), pp. 331–355.

Manovich, L. (2000). *The Language of New Media*. MIT Press: Cambridge, MA

Manovich, L. (2008). *Software Takes Command* http://lab.softwarestudies.com/2008/11/softbook.html

Mariampolski, H. (1999). The Power of Ethnography. *Journal of the Market Research Society*, 41 (1), p. 75.

Martin, J. A. (2014). Mobile media and political participation: Defining and developing an emerging field. *Mobile Media and Communication*, 2, pp. 173–195.

Marx, K. (1993). *Das Kapital, Vol. 3*. London: Penguin Classics.

Mascetti, S., Freni, D., Bettini, C., Wang, X. S., and Sushil, J. (2010), Privacy in geo-social networks: Proximity notification with untrusted service providers and curious buddies. *The VLDB Journal*, December 2010.

McCullough, M. (2006). On the urbanism of locative media. *Places*, 18 (2), pp. 26–29.

McHugh, K. E. (2007). Un-poetically "Man" dwells. *ACME: An International E-Journal for Critical Geographies*, 6 (2), pp. 258–277. Special issue: media spaces, mediated place.

McLuhan, M. (2008). *Understanding Media: The Extensions of Man*. New York: Penguin.

Meillassoux, Q. (2008). *After Finitude: An Essay on the Necessity of Contingency* (Trans. Brassier, R.). London: Continuum.

Merleau-Ponty, M. (2002). *The Phenomenology of Perception*. London: Routledge.

Merrin, W. (2014). The rise of the gadget and hyperludic me-dia. *Cultural Politics*, 10 (1), pp. 1–20.

Meyrowitz, J. (1985). *No Sense of Place: The Impact of Electronic Media on Social Behaviour*. Oxford University Press.

Michael, M. G. and Michael, K. (2009). *Uberveillance: Microchipping People and the Assault on Privacy*. http://ro.uow.edu.au/infopapers/711. Retrieved August 07, 2011.

Michael, K. and Michael, M. G. (2012). *Sousveillance and Point of View Technologies in Law Enforcement: An overview*. The Sixth Workshop on the Social Implications of National Security: Sousveillance and Point of View Technologies in Law Enforcement (An Overview). University of Sydney, NSW, Australia. February 2012.

Millard, M. and Soylu, F. (2009). *Use of Embodied Learning Approaches in Teaching Technology*. Paper presented at Association for Educational Communications and Technology (AECT) meeting, Louisville, KY: October 2009.

Miller, D. and Slater, D. (2001). *The Internet: An Ethnographic Approach*. Paris: Berg Publishers.

Miller, J. (2014). The fourth screen: Mediatization and the smartphone. *Mobile Media and Communication*, 2, pp. 209–228.

Mitsubishi Heritage (2010). http://global.mitsubishielectric.com/heritage/contents/gps/page_1.html. Retrieved June 02, 2010.

Moores, S. (2014). Digital Orientations: "Ways of the hand" and practical knowing in media uses and other manual activities. *Mobile Media and Communication*, 2, pp. 196–208.

Moran, D. (2000). *Introduction to Phenomenology* (1 ed.). New York: Routledge.

Morin, M-E. (2009). Cohabitating in the globalised world: Peter Sloterdijk's global foams and Bruno Latour's cosmopolitics. *Environment and Planning D: Society and Space*, 27 (1), pp. 58–72.

Mumford, L. (1934). *Technics and Civilisation*. New York: Harcourt, Brace & Company Inc.

Myers, T. (2001). The postmodern imaginary in William Gibson's Neuromancer. *MFS Modern Fiction Studies*, 47 (4), pp. 887–909.

Nagel, T. (1986). *The View from Nowhere*. Oxford: Oxford University Press.

Nelson, R. A. (1999). *The Global Positioning System: A National Resource*. Riva, Maryland: Applied Technology Institute. http://www.aticourses.com/global_positioning_system. Retrieved June 01, 2010

Nietzsche, F. (2003). *Beyond Good and Evil*. London: Penguin Classics.

O'Brien, M. (2004). Commentary on Heidegger's "the Question concerning technology. In A. Cashin and J. Jirsa (Ed.), *Thinking Together. Proceedings of the IWM Junior Fellows' Conference, Winter 2003*. Vienna: IWM Junior Visiting Fellows' Conferences, Vol. 16.

Okazaki, S. and Mendez, F. (2013). Perceived ubiquity in mobile services. *Journal of Interactive Marketing, 27*, pp. 98–111.

Oliver, R. (2005). *Ordnance Survey Maps: A Concise Guide for Historians (second edition)*. London: The Charles Close Society for the Study of the Ordnance Survey.

Olsson, G. (2007). *Abysmal: A Critique of Cartographic Reason*. Chicago: Chicago University Press.

Ozer, N. A., Conley, C., O'Connell, H., Ginsburg, E., and Gubins, T. (2010), *Location-based Services: Time for a Privacy Check-in*. ACLU of Northern California: San Francisco.

Parikka, J. (2012). Archives in media theory: Material media archaeology and digital humanities In D. M. Berry (Ed.), *Understanding Digital Humanities* (pp. 85–104). London: Palgrave Macmillan.

Parkinson, B. W. and Spilker, J. J. (1996). *The Global Positioning System: Theory and Applications*. New York: AIAA.

Paterson, M. (2007). *The Senses of Touch: Haptics, Affects and Technologies*. Oxford, UK: Berg.

Piccinini, G. (2007). Computing mechanisms. *Philosophy of Science*, 74, pp. 501–526.

Pioneer (2010). *History of Pioneer in the UK*. http://www.pioneer.co.uk/uk/content/company/company/history.html. Retrieved June 02, 2010.

Pollack, N. (2010). The great check-in battle. *Wired Magazine*, July 2010, pp. 90–98.

Popper, K. R. and Eccles, J. C. (2006). *The Self and its Brain: An Argument for Interactionism*. London: Routledge.

Portes, A. (1998). Social capital: Its origins and applications in modern sociology. *Annual Review of Sociology*, 24, pp. 1–24.

Postman, N. (1985). *Amusing Ourselves to Death: Public Discourse in the Age of Showbusiness*. New York: Penguin.

Prensky, M. (2001). Digital natives, digital immigrants. *On the Horizon*, 9 (5).

Putnam, R. D. (1995). Bowling alone: America's declining social capital. *Journal of Democracy*, 6 (1), pp. 64–78.

Pylyshyn, Z. W. (1989). Computing in cognitive science. In M. Posner (Ed.), *Foundations of Cognitive Science* (pp. 49–92). Cambridge: The MIT Press.

Rabinow, P. (1994). Modern and counter modern. In G. Gutting (Ed.),*The Cambridge Companion to Foucault* (pp. 197–214). Cambridge: Cambridge University Press.

Radloff, B. (2007). *Heidegger and the Question of National Socialism: Disclosure and Gestalt*. Toronto: University of Toronto Press.

Relph, E. (1976). *Place and Placelessness*. London: Pion.

Resnick, P. (2001). Beyond bowling together: Socio-technical capital. In J. Carroll (Ed.), *HCI in the New Millennium* (pp. 647–672). New York, NY: Addison-Wesley.

Richardson, I. (2008). Pocket technospaces: The bodily incorporation of mobile media. In G. Goggin (Ed.), *Mobile Phone Cultures* (pp. 66–76). London, UK: Routledge.

Richardson, I. (2012). Touching the screen: A phenomenology of mobile gaming and the iPhone. In L. Hjorth, J. Burgess and I. Richardson (Eds.), *Studying Mobile Media: Cultural Technologies, Mobile Communication and the iPhone* (pp. 133–154). New York, NY: Routledge.

Richardson, I. and Wilken, R. (2012). Parerga of the third screen: Mobile media, place, and presence. In R. Wilken and G. Goggin (Eds.), *Mobile Technology and Place* (pp. 181–197). New York, NY: Routledge.

Richardson, I. and Wilken, R. (2009). Haptic vision, footwork, place-making: A peripatetic phenomenology of the mobile phone pedestrian. *Second Nature*, 2, pp. 22–41.

Richardson, J. E. (2002). *Analysing Newspapers: An Approach from Critical Discourse Analysis*. Basingstoke: Palgrave Macmillan

Rip, M. R. and Hasik, J. M. (2002). *The Precision Revolution: GPS and the Future of Aerial Warfare*. Annapolis, MD: Naval Institute Press.

Rose, C. (2010). *The Security Implications of Ubiquitous Social Media*. 2010 EABR and ETLC Conference proceedings, Dublin, Ireland.

Rost, M., Cramer, H., Belloni, N., and Holmquist, L. E., (2010). *Geolocaion in the Mobile Web Browser*. Ubicomp 10 Proceedings of the 12th ACM international conference adjunct papers on Ubiquitous computing.

Roth, R. (2009). The challenges of mapping complex indigenous spatiality: From abstract space to dwelling space. *Cultural Geographies*, 16 (2), pp. 207–277.

Rybas, N. and Gajjala, R. (2007). Developing cyberethnographic research methods for understanding digitally mediated identities. *Forum Qualitative Sozialforschung/ Forum: Qualitative Social Research*, 8 (3) from http://www.qualitative-research. net/index.php/fqs/article/view/282/619. Retrieved February 02, 2011.

Sample, J. T. and Ioup, E. (2010). *Tile-based geospatial information systems: principles and practices*. New York: Springer.

Sartre, J-P. (1993). *Being And Nothingness*. New York: Washington Square Press.

Scannell, P. (1995). For a phenomenology of radio and television. *Journal of Communication*, 45, pp. 4–19.

Scheutz, M. (1999). When physical systems realize functions. *Minds and Machines*, 9, pp. 161–196.

Schinkel, W. and Noordegraaf-Eelens, L. (2011). Peter Sloterdijk's spherological acrobatics: An exercise in introduction. In *In Media Res:Peter Sloterdijk's Spherical Poetics of Being*. Amsterdam: Amsterdam University Press, pp.7–28.

Schonfeld, E. (2010). *It's Time for an Open Database of Places*. Techcrunch, http://techcrunch.com/2010/04/17/open-database-places. Retrieved June 01, 2010

Schwara, S. (1999). Ethnologie im zeichen von globalisierung und cyberspace. *Mitteilungen der Anthropologischen Gesellschaft in Wien (MAGW)*, 129, pp. 259–273.

Sennett, R. (2003). *Respect: the formation of character in a world of inequality*. London: Penguin.

Seymour, W. A. (Ed.) (1980). *A History of the Ordnance Survey*. London: Flip@once Digital Books.

Shaviro, S. (2010). *Post Cinematic Affect*. Ropely, Hants.: Zero Books.

Sheehan, T. (2007). *Heidegger, Martin (1889–1976)*. Routledge Encyclopaedia of Philosophy. http://www.stanford.edu/dept/relstud/faculty/sheehan/pdf/ Routledge.pdf. Retrieved December 12, 2008.

Sheller, M. (2004). Mobile Publics: Beyond the network perspective. *Environment and Planning D: Society and Space*, 22, pp. 39–52.

Shepard, M. (ed.) (2011). *Sentient City: Ubiquitous Computing, Architecture and the Future of Urban Space*. Cambridge, Mass.: MIT Press.

Shirky, C. (2010). *Cognitive Surplus: Creativity and Generosity in a Connected Age*. New York: Allen Lane.

Siegert, B. (2011). The Map is the Territory. *Radical Philosophy*, 169, pp. 13–16.

Silverman, M. (2011), Users for sale: Has digital illiteracy turned us into social commodities? *Mashable.com*, August 01, 2011, http://mashable.com/2011/06/30/users-products-rushkoff/. Retrieved July 10, 2011.

Singh, V. and Dickson, J. (2002). Ethnographic approaches to the study of organizations. In D. Partington (Ed.), *Essential Skills for Management Research*. Thousand Oaks, CA: Sage Publications Ltd.

Sloterdijk, P. (1998). *Sphären I – Blasen, Mikrosphärologie* [Spheres I – Bubbles, microspherology] (Suhrkamp, Frankfurt am Main)

Sloterdijk, P. (1999). *Sphären II – Globen, Makrosphärologie* [Spheres II – Globes, macrospherology] (Suhrkamp, Frankfurt am Main)

Sloterdijk, P. (2004). *Sphären III – Schäume, Plurale Sphärologie* [Spheres III – Bubbles, plural-spherology] (Suhrkamp, Frankfurt am Main)

Smith, B. C. (1996). *On the Origin of Objects*. Cambridge, MA: The MIT Press.

Smith, D. (1997). Phenomenology: Methodology and method. In J. Higgs (Ed.), *Qualitative Research: Discourse on methodologies* (pp. 75–80). Sydney, New South Wales, Australia: Hampden Press.

Smythe, D. W. (2006). On the audience commodity and its work. In *Media and Cultural Studies: Keyworks* (pp. 230–256). New York: Blackwell.

Steiner, G. (1978). *Heidegger (Modern Masters Series)*. London: Fontana.

Stiegler, B. (1998). *Technics and Time, 1: The Fault of Epimetheus*. Stanford: Stanford University Press.

Sutko, D. M. and de Souza e Silva, A. (2011). Location aware mobile media and urban sociability. *New Media & Society*, 13 (5), pp. 807–823.

ten Bos, R. (2009). Towards an amphibious anthropology: Water and Peter Sloterdijk, *Environment and Planning D: Society and Space*, 27 (1), pp. 73–86.

Thomas, J. (1993). *Doing Critical Ethnography*. Thousand Oaks, CA: Sage University.

Thomson, I (2005). *Heidegger on Ontotheology*. Cambridge: Cambridge University Press.

Thrift, N. (1996). *Spatial Formations*. London, UK: Sage.

Thrift, N. and French, S. (2002). The automatic production of space. *Transactions of the Institute of British Geographers*, 27 (3), pp. 309–335.

Tuan, Y. F. (1977). *Space and Place: The Perspective of Experience*. Minneapolis: University of Minnesota Press.

Turkle, S. (Ed.) (2007). *Evocative Objects: Things we Think With*. Cambridge: MIT Press.

Van Dijk, T. A. (ed.) (1997). *Discourse as Social Interaction*. London: Sage.

van Manen, M. (1997). *Researching Lived Experience: Human Science for an Action Sensitive Pedagogy* (2nd ed.). London, Ontario: Althouse press.

van Tuinen, S. (2009). Air conditioning spaceship earth: Peter Sloterdijk's ethico-aesthetic paradigm. *Environment and Planning D: Society and Space*, 27 (1), pp. 105–118.

Verhoeff, N. (2012). *Mobile Screens: The Visual Regime of Navigation*. Amsterdam: Amsterdam University Press.

Vitak, J. and Ellison, N. (2013). "There's a network out there you might as well tap": Exploring the benefits of and barriers to exchanging informational and support-based resources on Facebook. *New Media & Society*, 15, pp. 243–259.

Wilken, R. (2008). Mobilising Place: Mobile Media, Peripatetics, and the Renegotiation of Urban Places, *Journal of Urban Technology*, 15 (3), pp. 39–55.

Wilken, R. (2011). *Teletechnologies, Place, and Community*. New York: Routledge.

Wilken, R. (2011). Bonds and Bridges: Mobile Phones and Social Capital Debates. In Ling, R. and Campbell, S. (Eds.), *Mobile Communication: Bringing Us Together and Tearing Us Apart*. New Brunswick, NJ: Transaction Publishers. pp. 127–149.

Wilken, R. (2012). Locative media: From specialized preoccupation to mainstream fascination, *Convergence*, 18, pp. 243–247.

Williams, R. (2003). *Technology and Cultural Form*. London: Psychology Press.

Wrathall, M. (2006). *How to Read Heidegger (How to Read)*. New York: W. W. Norton.

Yang, S., Kurnia, S., and Smith, S. (2011). *The Impact of Mobile Phone Use on Individual Social Capital*, Hawaii International Conference on System Sciences, January 5–8, 2011, Kauai, Hawai

Young, J. (2000). What is dwelling? The homelessness of modernity and the worlding of the world. In H. L. Dreyfus, M. A. Wrathall, and J. E.Malpas (Eds.), *Heidegger, Authenticity, and Modernity: Essays in Honor of Hubert L. Dreyfus* (pp. 187–204). Cambridge, Mass.: MIT Press.

Young, J. (2006) The Fourfold. In C. B. Guignon (Ed.), *The Cambridge companion to Heidegger (2nd Edition)*. Cambridge: Cambridge University Press.

Zichermann, G. and Cunningham, C. (2011). *Gamification by Design: Implementing Game Mechanics in Web and Mobile Apps*. Sebastopol, CA: O'Reilly Media.

Index